Highway to Learning
Lessons from a
Lifelong Learning Network

Highway to Learning
Lessons from a
Lifelong Learning Network

edited by

Lynn Benton and Nick Hooper

LIBRI
PUBLISHING

First published in 2010 by Libri Publishing

ISBN 978 1 907471 11 7

A CIP catalogue record for this book is available from The British Library

Cover design by Helen Taylor
Page design by Carnegie Publishing

Printed in the UK by Ashford Colour Press Ltd

Libri Publishing
Brunel House
Volunteer Way
Faringdon
Oxfordshire
SN7 7YR

Tel: +44 (0)845 873 3837

www.libripublishing.co.uk

This book is dedicated to Lola Rose
who entered the world in time to be
the youngest member of our team
and a future lifelong learner.

Acknowledgements

Many people were involved in the story of YHELLN (Yorkshire & Humber East Lifelong Learning Network). We cannot name them all here, but we can and do acknowledge their contribution.

As well as the YHELLN staff named as authors, a number of other people worked alongside us during the three years of the project. Our work benefited greatly from the efforts of Support Officers in each partner institution: Kim Routledge in YHELLN itself, Caroline Beasley (University of Hull), Dawn King (Grimsby Institute of Further and Higher Education), Kate Murdock (East Riding College), Daniel Munnings (Selby College), Laura Minghella (Yorkshire Coast College), Lynda Burton (Doncaster College) and Kate Cockerill (North Lindsey College). Sue Cordell acted as YHELLN Quality Officer during the first two years of the project. Liz Hunt led the Health, Education and Social Care Higher Skills team before handing over to Rob Creasy. Katie Alsop joined us in the final year to help with publicity and events.

The driving force behind the establishment of YHELLN was Graham Chesters, at the time Pro Vice Chancellor of the University of Hull. Graham left shortly after the formation of YHELLN and thus bears no responsibility for what we made of his vision. Our efforts have, therefore, been guided by a Steering Group and led by a Management Group. We thank them for their work on our behalf.

Our greatest thanks go to the many people in our partners and beyond who learnt with us on the YHELLN journey and who will continue what they helped us to start. This is as much their story as ours. Yorkshire & Humberside East is indeed fortunate to have such a group of dedicated and inspiring professionals supporting vocational higher education across the region.

Out last thanks are to Don Knibb and John Alibone whose track changes and red ink mean that this book, hopefully, will be in 'Queen's English' and make sense to our readers.

The views expressed in this book are those of the authors and do not necessarily reflect the views of YHELLN or its partners.

Contents

Foreword

'Next in importance to freedom and justice is popular education, without which neither freedom nor justice can be permanently maintained.'

These noble words were spoken by James A Garfield, the 20th President of the United States of America.

I studied the life of President Garfield, the second of four US Presidents to be assassinated, during my BA Honours studies in London in the early 1980s.

I was fortunate to come from a home where a degree-level education was an expectation, not an aspiration; a pre-determined journey carefully mapped out by parents and teachers in a way that would have made the Ordnance Survey proud.

The complexities of the current education system fascinated me, even before I was asked to play a small part in the YHELLN project.

The training company I run had diversified into the provision of work based learning focused on the media and I had encountered young learners for the first time in 25 years. It was clear to me that more had to be done to help learners navigate a pathway to achievement through the various choices that lay before them. So when I was invited to chair this Lifelong Learning Network's Steering Group, as an independent, employer representative, it was an easy decision to accept the offer.

It has been a fascinating three years. Not always easy, not without challenges, but ultimately, successful in many areas, including progression between courses.

This is entirely down to the hard work and dedication of the management team, led by Jenny Shaw and her officers, and the cooperation of the partners.

This book is a notable record of the success and achievements of YHELLN as it hands its work to the Hull University Federation.

Tony Johnston

Head of Press Association Training

December 2009

Introduction

....

Lynn Benton and Nick Hooper

For a number of years, belief in the knowledge economy as the way forward for the UK has been a cornerstone of UK government policy and part of the accepted mantra of all major political parties. This has spawned a plethora of reports into its meaning and implementation and a succession of policy initiatives designed to make it happen.

Among these policy initiatives has been support for vocational higher education, defined as Level 4 or first-year university and above. Vocational HE is seen as a neglected, but essential, aspect of the HE of the future. The creation of Lifelong Learning Networks (LLNs) was one of the practical outcomes of these policies.

This book is the story of a three-year project to improve access to vocational higher education in the eastern part of the Yorkshire & Humber region of the UK. It describes the impediments to vocational higher education identified by the HE providers (colleges and University) working together as the Yorkshire & Humber East Lifelong Learning Network (YHELLN) and the initiatives developed, introduced and applied to overcome those barriers.

From the start, YHELLN had a dual personality. On the one hand, YHELLN refers to the staff who worked directly for YHELLN and who are the authors of this book. On the other hand, YHELLN relates to the wider partnership of academic institutions and stakeholders. As a result, in the chapters which follow, YHELLN can relate to the staff of YHELLN or to the partnership.

Structure of the book

The authors were each given a brief to write an essay telling the story as they saw it, setting out the important issues and outcomes in their area. The editors have made no attempt to standardise the essays, which were produced to meet the brief. As a result, there is a variety of styles and approaches illustrated in the chapters that follow.

Jenny Shaw, Director of YHELLN, and Andrew Chandler, YHELLN Communications Manager, set out the background to LLNs and the YHELLN approach in Chapter 1. This is followed by an overview of vocational HE by Jenny Shaw in Chapter 2.

A series of chapters written by the staff of YHELLN responsible for managing activity in specific areas starts with three key activities: curriculum development (Chapter 3, Karen Quine, Work Strand Manager for Curriculum Development); progression agreements (Chapter 4, Charlie Sanders, Work Strand Manager for Progression); and learner support, information advice and guidance (Chapter 5, Jane Barker, Work Strand Manager for Learner Support).

These are followed by chapters reflecting examples of YHELLN's over-arching activity: In Chapter 6 Jane Barker and Kelly McDonald (Project Officer, YHELLN and Higher York) describe work on labour market information. Sarah Gribbin (Higher Skills Team Leader for Business & Logistics) explores the issues involved when HEIs work with business in Chapter 7.

As well as themed work strands, YHELLN identified and established priority curriculum areas, each with a Higher Skills Team Leader. Each Higher Skills Team Leader sets out the YHELLN experience of good practice in their curriculum area: Sarah Gribbin for business & logistics (Chapter 8), Sarah Humphreys for creative arts (Chapter 9), John Deverell for engineering & construction (Chapter 10). As a result of staff changes, there is no chapter for the fourth curriculum priority sector, health, education and social care.

There follow two chapters setting out the contribution of support strands: Nick Hooper, Work Strand Manager for Research, CPD and Evaluation, outlines the contribution of the YHELLN research programme in Chapter

11 and David Sowden, E-Systems Manager, and Jason Reed, Consultant, describe the role of e-systems in the YHELLN story in Chapter 12.

Chapter 13 reviews the lessons learnt for the progression of vocational learners and for the wider community for lifelong learners from the perspective of Kath Bridger, Consultant and YHELLN Strategic Lead between July and December 2008.

The book concludes with a postscript written by Glen Jack, YHELLN Management accountant, in which Glen reflects on his experience of working for YHELLN from a professional and personal perspective. While the details may differ, all those who formed part of the YHELLN team can identify with Glen's story.

YHELLN met or exceeded all of its targets as set out in the Business Plans. Those who believed in the YHELLN initiative and helped to make it happen recognised that the Business Plan targets and deliverables were only part of the story – the measurable indicators of achievement and justification of the resources. The true aim of YHELLN and the outcome against which we would wish to be judged was cultural change – the creation of a culture in which partners work together to place vocational (and other) learners at the centre and in control of their learning. There are no statistical indicators which measure our success against this aim. This book celebrates our view of the achievements of the YHELLN partners during a unique three-year experiment. We hope it allows you to take up from where we finished and continue to look for better ways to support lifelong learning, wherever, with whomever and for whatever reason it happens.

CHAPTER ONE
YHELLN

Jenny Shaw and Andrew Chandler

Conceived at a time when Britain was enjoying sustained economic growth, Lifelong Learning Networks (LLNs) reflected a general mood of optimism as well as a desire to widen participation in higher education (HE). The rationale was simple. If we encourage people to make the most of their talents, we improve the skill level of the population and our ability to compete in a global economy. The challenge has been to reach out to those who were not persuaded by the benefits of continuing their education or who, for a number of reasons, have in the past been unable to grasp the opportunities that have existed.

The argument for establishing a network was compelling and followed Lord Dearing's proposals on the future of higher education, published more than a decade ago and the Review of Skills, carried out by Lord Leitch in 2006. Both identified a future in which higher education and higher skills were the essential ingredients of a modern economy.

In common with most other networks, the Yorkshire & Humber East Lifelong Learning Network (YHELLN), established in January 2007, was funded by the Higher Education Funding Council for England (HEFCE) for a three-year period. The initial business plan, drawn up in consultation with partners, followed an expression of interest submitted to HEFCE in 2005. The focus was on how YHELLN could take to a different level the existing collaboration that characterised the relationship between Further Education Colleges in the East of the Yorkshire and Humber region and the University of Hull. The Humber Higher Education Strategic Framework, agreed in 2004 by all institutions represented on the Humber HE Council, provided a broad strategic base on which to build and extend membership to include other partners, including Higher York.

At the heart of the network and fundamental to its success has been the notion of enhanced progression opportunities for vocational learners. The many barriers that influence participation in HE are well documented. Many are cultural or financial and, due to the initiative's three year timescale, we recognised that there were several upon which YHELLN could not hope to have any positive impact. However, we believe that the higher education system and the way in which it operates locally, should not in itself be one of the barriers and this challenge was something over which we could perhaps exert some influence. This became our mission and a strong, guiding principle from the very beginning and throughout the life of YHELLN.

Much of our work has, therefore, been about influencing the design and development of systems that in turn impact upon the take-up of higher education by vocational learners. Furthermore and crucially, from the outset we recognised the need to ensure that whatever difference we could make had to be given the best possible chance of lasting beyond the life of YHELLN. Embedding good practice and focusing upon sustainable development, when initiatives were conceived and funding allocated, formed part of our ideology.

It may seem axiomatic, but it is nevertheless worth remembering that it is people who make things happen – they make the important decisions, influence others and effect change. YHELLN's communications strategy had to reflect this and the fact that our delivery partners are the ones who will continue to have direct contact with potential learners in the future.

The approach to YHELLN's marketing activities can therefore be summed up as 'Business to Business' network or relationship marketing. Our aim has been to communicate a clear set of messages to our direct partners and to wider stakeholders who have an influence on our key target group of vocational learners seeking to move into and through higher education.

As a change programme, communication is at the heart of what we have set out to do and, ultimately, achieved. Our resources of £4M over three years were clearly not sufficient to set up an entire infrastructure for managing the progression of vocational learners across the partnership as a whole and, even if they had been, such a venture would not have been sustainable. Rather, our task was to test and refine systems, demonstrate their effectiveness and value, model new ways of working and provide capacity building interventions, all the time focusing on the long term benefit to our target group.

In order to do this effectively we have had to manage two areas of work. The first has been the most tangible – we have ourselves had to carry out or otherwise procure the programme of pilots, systems development and capacity building activities. This has meant leading and managing a programme of individual projects and interventions. The second area has probably been hidden to the majority of the partners and stakeholders but has been no less crucial. We have had to undertake a substantial and planned programme of engagement and communication. This 'shadow side' of the initiative has been essential for a number of reasons linked to the different life stages of YHELLN.

It was important for us to set out our stall in the early months with strong, clear messages about our vision and intentions. We did this through a number of measures. We developed a distinctive branding, destined to have a short 'shelf life' but with an immediate imperative to represent the vision and values of the lifelong learning network and that of our partners. Of equal and increasing importance as the network matured was the introduction of the 'Highway' brand, a generic or umbrella 'product' brand, representing vocational higher education that was introduced and adopted by a number of partners. This provided us with a cost-effective method for promoting opportunities for vocational learners, creating a strategic link across different initiatives and acting as a banner for associated campaigns and activities funded or co-funded by YHELLN. These two branding exercises have been important in order to keep the mission of YHELLN high in the consciousness of partners and stakeholders and, therefore, to keep the issue of vocational progression and vocational higher education high on everyone's agenda.

Our brand has gone far beyond the simple creation of a logo. From the earliest stages the team was agreed on the need to promote a single clear message, for which we adopted the strapline 'increasing opportunities for vocational learners in higher education'. Our visual identity, including the use of accent colours, has emphasised this message and allowed it to permeate our work and that of the partners.

A secondary objective was to promote values that we hoped would challenge the negative image and low aspirations of the sub-region. We wanted to demonstrate a brand that was distinctive and striking, to emphasise our high expectations and belief in excellence, opportunity and possibility.

Following the branding of YHELLN, we focused our efforts on creating interest and excitement through a number of key events of which our launch was an important part. We were fortunate to secure Alan Johnson, the MP for Hull West and Hessle and then Secretary of State, to speak at this event. Through speeches and our launch video our aim was to build on work already happening within the partnership to set out an ambitious but achievable vision for opportunity and clarity for vocational learners and closer engagement between the higher education and business communities.

Communication is about both imparting and receiving information. But to be most effective, we needed to ensure that our messages in the first eighteen months represented a 'call to action' that would stimulate partners and stakeholders to get involved and to contribute their skills, experience and perspectives. This was important as in those first months we were quite clear that staff in the partner organisations were the ones who were closest to the real issues we sought to address and who had some of the answers we were seeking. Drawing out this expertise and 'tacit knowledge' therefore was the impetus behind a call for project proposals. Our hope was that the promise of funding would be a strong stimulant and we were not wrong! However, alongside this, senior members of the team were working hard with the movers and shakers within the partnership and wider stakeholder group to identify long term 'business benefits' to the types of activity we were championing. Larger and more reliable inflows of well prepared students, opportunities to refresh course portfolios and sharing the costs of development activities, including employer engagement, were all attractive propositions and we promoted these potential benefits strongly. We were building for the future, setting the foundations of what we hoped would be a sustainable programme that would continue beyond the initial tranche of funding simply because it met partners' needs as providers of higher education.

Among our wider stakeholders we relentlessly promoted the benefits of higher level skills to the local economy and the wellbeing of the local population. By association, this was a promotion of the role higher education providing organisations could play in regeneration. In essence, where there were conversations about the benefits of higher vocational skills, the case for HE could be made. The aim has been to encourage people to talk about higher skills in the region, creating opportunities for 'conversations' about higher learning, and to influence the outcomes of those conversations and ultimately behaviour, in line with our vision. An example of this was the campaign we ran on 'World Class Skills' during the spring and summer of 2008. Although the message ultimately had to be adapted to deal with the drastically changing economic situation, we did succeed in bringing together a broad range of partners, including local authority elected members, to talk positively about the potential of the city-region and the contribution of higher education to achieving that potential.

The latter half of the project, and particularly the last year, has been about making change stick. We have sought out examples of effective practice that have demonstrated their impact and effectiveness, and championed these relentlessly. Our aim has been to encourage 'copy cat' initiatives across the partnership and while we have pump-primed some of these, a better measure of our success has been where partners have resourced these themselves. Progression interventions built around accredited 'bridging' modules have been a prime example of this, brought about in part by our decision to ask senior staff to champion successful projects from their own institutions at YHELLN Management Group meetings.

To drive the process of change even deeper and to ensure that lessons learned were captured for future use, we have chosen to commit significant resources to dissemination across the whole of the final year. Our 'all the best' good practice guides have sought to articulate practical know-how illustrated by examples, and this has been followed up with a conference of the same name. Alongside these more obvious communications, there has also been a strong push on person-to-person communication, with all YHELLN team members acting as champions, not for YHELLN per se, but for good and effective practice and for the benefits of partnership working.

Throughout the entire lifecycle of YHELLN, the role of the staff as individual communicators and catalysts has perhaps been underestimated, even by us. While we have a small directorate, the bulk of our team has been embedded within the different partner organisations. These staff members have often continued within their previous roles on a part time basis, but at the same time have been a part of something bigger. They have each taken forward key areas of work across the entire partnership, exposing them to different people, approaches and ways of thinking. This in turn has allowed them to bring contacts and opportunities into their home institutions and to inform others about the wider picture. Furthermore, within their areas of expertise all staff have found themselves giving some level of coaching, either through structured staff development sessions or more commonly on a one-to-one basis with people they were advising or supporting. This aspect of our communications, we believe, has enabled us to achieve the deep and long lasting changes to on-the-ground practice that are now being reported as part of our impact assessment.

Promoting the YHELLN brand has been a balancing act between seeking to ensure that our various stakeholders, including HEFCE, appreciated the impact that the network has had on increased 'take-up' on the one hand and remaining in the background on the other – recognising that a public face was inappropriate for the reasons described above. We were the catalyst. The true test of the effectiveness and impact of our work will be whether initiatives continue without us, because we were able to broker and demonstrate the value of partnership.

CHAPTER TWO

Vocational HE

Jenny Shaw

Vocational education has famously been described as 'a great idea for other people's children'. (Wolf, 2002) In 1977, talking about vocational and technical education, Paul Willis wrote: 'The working class view would be the rational one were it not located in a class society, i.e. that theory is only useful insofar as it really does help to do things... For the middle class, more aware of its position in a class society, however, theory is seen partly in its social guise of qualifications as the power to move up the social scale. In this sense theory is well worth having even if it is never applied to nature.' (Willis, 1977) In doing so, I believe he summed up the main issue facing learners in the UK who choose a vocational learning route. Vocational learning has long been a devalued form of learning in this country; a route for the 'less able' or for 'non-traditional' students, because it is associated with the working class and working-class values. Academic learning, on the other hand, is a route into a broad spectrum of professional and managerial occupations and a marker of the middle class. In the days of grammar schools, an academic education was a potential route for social mobility, for leaving one's class behind and transforming into something else. And yet still in the 21st century many of us feel we are still fighting a battle against the 'final frontier' of class inequality in education.

However, perhaps the tide is turning. I believe that an important battle was won in the hearts and minds of policy makers when it was recognised that educational equality does not simply mean more people doing what the middle classes have traditionally done well – slotting into a system of higher education that represents the values, background and 'cultural capital' (to cite Bourdieu) of one particular section of society.

Rather, it means valuing learning and development in a range of forms, including challenging the increasingly outmoded distinction between vocational and academic education which is so deeply classed. It also means changing the way we think as educationalists – from the language we use to describe learners, to the beliefs we hold about the abilities of students because of their background, to the norms that we take for granted about the 'correct' way to learn and express learning at higher level, through to our very philosophy about concepts such as meritocracy and entitlement.

In setting out his vision for the Lifelong Learning Networks programme, Sir Howard Newby stated that 'if higher education is not adequately prepared to accommodate today's vocational learners this reflects deeply ingrained cultural hostility to too close an association between intelligence and its application'. (Newby, 2005) Thus, in the early 21st century a programme was announced that tackled the very issue identified by Paul Willis in the 1970s. Not only should vocational education not be a barrier to progression into higher education, but vocational higher education can and should be possible as an integral and equal part of our tertiary system. The programme would be realised by bringing together groups of providers – primarily further and higher education institutions – on a local, sub-regional or regional basis to address these issues in partnership.

Looking back, it is perhaps easy to forget the experimental spirit in which this programme was launched. Both in the article cited above and in the Colin Bell Memorial Lecture in which LLNs were announced, many more questions and issues were raised than answered. With the skills strategy still at an early stage and employer engagement in higher education barely on the radar, the call to arms was for innovative solutions in order to 'make the whole HE offer available to learners over a lifetime of work and study, allowing people to build on their earlier learning without being confined by it'.

Lifelong Learning Networks, therefore, were intended to be 'pilots and demonstrators' (HEFCE) addressing a broad sweep of issues. They were intended to be large scale experiments. Some aspects might not work; others could model the way forward on a much wider scale. They were also meant to be catalysts for change or rather, as I often said in the early months, to support institutions in dealing with change that was coming upon them anyway.

The concept of progression has been at the heart of our Network, as with many, and this is the area in which, I believe, we have seen the most change. I am able to look back on the conversations I had with staff at all levels in partner organisations in the early days of YHELLN and compare them with the feedback we are now receiving three years on. Crucially, I have seen attitudes move from progression in a passive sense, or at best as an extension of standard student recruitment activities, to an active understanding of the needs and interest of students from a range of backgrounds and how these might be met. 'Students know they can progress' or 'it's very clear in the prospectus' were comments I heard in the first couple of months in post. In common with most other LLNs I've spoken to, it took some time for us to demonstrate that for some students this wasn't quite enough.

For me the key to understanding why this should be lies within a small body of sociological research around issues of higher education and social class. In their seminal text, Louise Archer and her colleagues argue that decision-making about progression to higher education is not a single moment of decision, nor is it necessarily a rational one. (Archer et al, 2003; Hutchings, 2003) Rather, it is contextual and above all strongly classed. Without doing violence to a complex and subtle argument, two factors stand out. Firstly, that young working-class people lack a sense of entitlement to higher education that their middle-class peers take for granted and, secondly, that tailored information provided by a known and trusted party (for example a tutor) is significantly more relevant, valued and likely to be acted on than publicly available sources of general information. (Ball, 1998)

Progression agreements and the activities that surround them have the potential to address both of these issues, and this is why I am increasingly of the opinion that they are not only desirable but essential in waging this war against educational inequalities. Progression agreements, even in the form of a simple, single page document, make it very clear to individual students that higher education is something to which they are personally entitled. This is 'official' information produced at institutional level and yet it is strongly contextualised to an individual student's circumstances. It states that people *on this course* are entitled and indeed encouraged to progress to higher education if they meet certain requirements for attainment. This is a world away from a general offer in a prospectus, because it means, for the learner, that *people like me* can and do progress. Not just people a bit like me – abstract categories such as vocational learners – but people exactly like me, people within my own course and cohort. It suddenly becomes a permissible aspiration.

However, as most people will realise, there is far more to a progression agreement than simply a piece of paper. Progression agreements start with talking – sometimes lots of it. I know that some of our partners have used progression agreements as a Trojan horse to get closer to their partners, to give them a focus for discussion and to give some shape to future partnership working. This appears to have been effective both within and outside the core partnership, opening the door to a wide range of new relationships with, for example, schools, work-based learning providers and professional bodies.

There is also a need to look in detail at curriculum and course offering – what the sensible next step might be for a learner on a particular programme, whether progression opportunities exist, whether there are unnecessary barriers in the way of progression, whether an entitlement to progress can and should exist and whether students are ever told about this. Sometimes these discussions have taken place internally to a partner institution and have resulted in the development of new HE opportunities and/or the articulation of internal progression routes. In other cases, groups of partners have worked together to rationalise some sensible opportunities for local learners and to make sure they are genuinely accessible to those who are sufficiently motivated to achieve.

In other instances, perceived gaps have been filled in innovative ways. For example bite-size modules have acted as a bridge into higher education for those previously learning in the community or the workplace, giving not only tasters and confidence, but valuable skills and knowledge to help them in their future studies. Our pilot APEL work and the 'HE for Me' programme are likely to play a similar role.

Finally, there is the need to make sure that learners are professionally informed and advised about issues of progression, whether through YHELLN progression agreements or opportunities in institutions and programmes throughout the UK. Thus information, advice and guidance throughout the learning journey become an important part of the offer. YHELLN invested in human capital and technical infrastructure to ensure that information, advice and guidance will continue over the coming years.

Lifelong learning networks were not intended to be delivery programmes, nor were they meant to set up a firm and solid infrastructure. Had they been funded over a longer period of time, or perhaps granted a second tranche of funding, I believe they would, like Aimhigher, have gone on to deliver a more regularised programme of interventions. But this was never the intention. They were meant to apply some innovative thinking to a longstanding problem. In doing so, I believe they were meant to catalyse the process of change, not least by sensitising the sector to the issues, but also by modelling good practice and perhaps also by demonstrating which routes to avoid at all costs!

It will probably be obvious by this point that presiding over such a large-scale experiment with so little guidance and even less precedent is likely to put one in a fairly tenuous position. Carrying out a change project is difficult at the best of times, but when the change is centrally driven rather than locally, and when it takes place in such turbulent times, it can be very difficult to know what success is meant to look like and whether the success will be welcomed if it occurs. It is perhaps not surprising that a number of Networks have chosen to run as delivery projects, or have set up infrastructures with separate and distinct identities and activities. In such cases it is relatively easy to measure what has been done, what has been gained, and to tell a good story in terms of 'value for money'.

We chose to do something different, guided I may say by advice from HEFCE. While I am naturally interested in those learners who have directly benefited from activities within the Network – and there are many – I am more interested in those who will continue to benefit for years to come – for I am starting to see change. Progression, a concept that until recently brought blank stares, now means something to many people within the partnership. What's more, they know what to do about it. The team is now regularly approached for advice on a broad range of issues around progression from on-the-ground practitioners across the Network, and the feedback we are receiving as projects and initiatives come to an end is about a permanent change. There are many instances in which partners have committed to continue funding progression and engagement activities, having now demonstrated, through YHELLN funding, that they are viable and beneficial. Sometimes the changes are smaller, but no less radical. For a department that has never before given systematic thought to the recruitment of vocational learners, sitting down at a meeting with a partner to discuss a possible progression agreement represents a paradigm shift. In both cases, real opportunities are created for those typically less likely to progress. To put it bluntly, they represent new opportunity for working-class learners.

A question I am beginning to be asked now that we are approaching the end of our funded life is whether I think we have achieved value for money. I'm not really sure how to answer this. Partly this is because, given that we set out to deliver a change project rather than deliver a programme, we will not have all the required evidence for many years to come. Partly it is because I'm a scientific realist rather than an empiricist and we tend to be a bit annoying like that. There is also the question of whose value for whose money. The funding was from HEFCE and, though the guidance was fluid, there were certain boundaries and requirements. Certainly the value was meant to be primarily for learners rather than institutions, and there was an explicit focus on progression, alongside implicit ones around the uneasy bedfellows of class equality and the skills agenda.

However, I do think we have succeeded in adding value. Change has happened; some of it we have caused but far more of it we have facilitated. These changes make it more likely for vocational learners to progress, ergo value is added. I know this latter fact to be true, by the way, because progression to the University of Hull from YHELLN members has often doubled and in one case trebled on our watch, while non-members have not seen such a change.

When I originally interviewed for the post of Director of YHELLN, I stated that my own success criterion would be that I would be out of a job in three years' time, because the change process would have picked up sufficient momentum to carry on under its own steam. There is a cautionary tale here and one should be careful what one wishes for! But if it means that other working-class young people can like me, through education, escape the council estates, travel a little, live a little and enjoy professional success, then it was a job well done.

CHAPTER THREE

Curriculum Development

Karen Quine and Lynn Benton

Times are changing, and the higher education curriculum must meet the needs of potential students who are increasingly likely to be already in employment or have family commitments and have vocational qualifications rather than A-Levels. Increasingly, learners are paying for the HE experience and, as a result, are becoming more demanding customers. With this in mind it is critical for higher education to ensure that its curriculum offer is fit for purpose and appeals to the target audience.

Adapting the curriculum to continue to meet the needs of students and at the same time the government's requirements for higher education is a huge task and one that YHELLN has been committed to supporting. The main concerns for curriculum development were:

- How degrees and foundation degrees prepare students for employment, especially with local companies

- How higher education meets the direct, higher level training and organisational development needs of employers

- How higher education is offered in such a way that it is accessible to a wide range of potential students with differing needs and backgrounds.

This chapter describes the strategic background and context for curriculum development and includes a summative review of one response to these needs: a pragmatic curriculum development model known as Staged Engagement.

> Education entails more than packaging and delivering knowledge to passive customers. Students play a more active and integral part in their own educational process. (Franz 1998)

Although this was written over a decade ago, never has its resonance been truer than in the 21st century. Today we are faced with ever more sophisticated 'customers'; ones who understand fitness for purpose and freedom of choice; customers who will either engage, because what is offered fits with their wants and needs, or ones who will not, because it does not match their expectations and their perceptions of value for money.

The challenge now is threefold. We need collaboration between HE providers and employers, agreement on the role of higher education in developing the UK workforce and acceptance of the need for cultural change by both parties to meet the 2020 targets. Practitioners and HE providers need to be more creative in marketing and promoting training and development: not just selling it as a commodity. We cannot assume because the government funds and HE providers supply, that the service is perceived as a benefit to employers. New methods and models of employer engagement need to be considered, to balance and facilitate the engagement with 'employers', contextualised to their needs, and we must engender and deliver a curriculum model which allows for progression through the educational milieu.

This recent emphasis on vocational skills and responsiveness to employer demands for relevant skills calls for new modes of delivery and a customer-led (market-led) approach to be taken by education institutions.

The crucial issue here is that strategic curriculum planning cannot be executed without considering the segment of the market at which the curriculum is aimed. Doyle (1998) makes the point that 'segmentation is the key to marketing because it offers the firm the chance to meet customer needs more effectively and build sales growth and profit.' The principles of marketing – being customer led, effective segmentation and sound planning – will remain fundamental to successful organisations in the years ahead.

If HE providers are serious about engaging with employers, they must be flexible and responsive and actively target segments of the employer groups. The Department for Innovation, Universities and Skills in their response to the Leitch Review: World Class Skills, states that:

> Treating employers and individual learners as the customers of the skills system is central to the idea of a demand-led approach.

This, however, assumes that HE providers are able and indeed want to employ business techniques to engage with employers. Many HE providers do not have a totally clear, well-established view of market requirements. For any knowledge exchange and brokerage system to be suitable, a clear strategic partnership needs to be formed between education providers and market segments of employers.

One way that the government has tried to achieve this is by the financial incentivisation of participation in training. As Johnson (2002) states:

> If policy makers are to succeed in ensuring that the skill needs of the economy are met, they need to persuade and/or incentivise employers to invest in people while also convincing individuals to invest in their own learning.

The government has, to a large extent, followed Johnson's advice in a dual attempt to target skills training at the employer and employee. The Bolton Report (1971) stated that any educational/ training provision to businesses should be in response to market demand and that training should be neither free nor subsidised, otherwise firms would not value it. Within the higher education sector there remains a reliance on funding subsidies for training and education.

Incentives to businesses today still tend to consist of free or co-funded training provision. The fundamental issue, however, is employers' understanding of the need for a skills base, but also – on a deeper level – understanding of the importance of training for business needs: linking training and development to wider strategic implications for organisational development and competitiveness.

This need would appear to be borne out by John Denham, (2007), Secretary of State for Innovation, Universities and Skills, with his policy agenda for World Class Skills. Employers need proof of the benefits from investing in learning.

> Policy makers and learning providers tend to assume that involvement in training and learning activities will automatically and unambiguously lead to economic benefits for employers. (Johnson 2002)

The approach adopted in response to Denham has been to encourage higher education providers to adapt by working in partnership. Should the HE providers accept the challenge, rise to the occasion and enter into genuine partnerships with employers, it may be expected that it will be the large employers and consortia that will be effectively engaged. Larger employers are already responding to training and development, often with dedicated personnel employed specifically for the purpose. For the HE provider to engage and work in partnership with such groups is less resource intensive and is more likely to lead to positive partnership development. As a result, employer engagement has been successful with many larger national and multi-national employers. In other words, these employers are largely switched on to the benefits of training and development and organisational development. Perhaps if the government really wants to see employers as part of the World Class Skills agenda, they should be facilitating and enabling this engagement under a widening participation agenda with committed and credible resources for employer engagement and development.

It is in this context that YHELLN developed an appropriate, flexible and pragmatic model to address the multi-faceted nature of engaging both non-traditional learners and employers in education, training and development. The model, known as 'Staged Engagement', is a way to engage learners and employers in demand-led programmes.

The essence of staged engagement is that learners, and particularly learners new to HE, do not have to commit to a long programme of study at the outset. Learning at HE level can start with a short 'taster' or master-class session lasting a few hours. Progression can be by stages through modules, or a short course award which may lead to a full qualification.

The point of the model is that it is not fixed but flexible and responds to the employer/learner needs without having to commit to a full qualification. It is about engagement of learners, employers and sponsors in demand-led progression: a moveable feast of expert sessions, bite-size modules, foundation degrees and beyond.

The YHELLN staged engagement support for partners included:

- University of Hull validated modules

- Visits to partners to develop appropriate and relevant, quality assurance modules

- Involvement of employers in the curriculum

- A handbook to inform and advise the developers through each stage of the process

- Assistance with marketing and promotional activities

- A module-focused evaluation questionnaire to check the effectiveness of the programme from the learners' perspective, and to influence future developments.

The aim of the model is to balance and facilitate the demands of the employers, the needs of the employees/learners and the higher skills requirements of the area. This is achieved by engendering and delivering a generic model whilst allowing for differing practices within each institution and embedding strategically staged engagement.

YHELLN was approached by Aimhigher (Humber) to facilitate their 'Master-Classes/Expert Sessions' initiative. The aim of the initiative was to encourage 'non-traditional' learners to consider vocationally orientated, higher education by running short (two hour) taster sessions on a variety of subjects within YHELLN's priority learning areas; business and logistics, health, education and social care, creative arts and engineering and construction.

The 'expert sessions', as they are locally called, are flexible in the delivery, timing, cost, topic and target audience. The sessions start to engage learners and/or employers in a developmental, two hour session, in demand-led programmes without the need to commit to full qualification. What is important is that the target audience considers it to be of sufficient value to commit one or two hours of their time to gather information, be stimulated and have thoughts provoked.

Also of paramount importance are the clearly articulated progression routes that could be followed as a natural progression from the initial expert session; for example, a 10/15 credit HE Level 4 'bite-size' module.

This provides a conduit for employers to support employees to learn more about the subject area. The 10/15 credit module can be supplemented with subsequent 10/15 credit modules and build towards a full award within the awarding academic institution, should they wish.

YHELLN has facilitated two models of staged engagement. The first has been directly linked to the 32 Additional Student Numbers (ASNs) franchised by the university. These have been used by colleges in either specific curriculum areas, such as digital media, or more as a progression aid, for example, in the delivery of study support skills modules. The second model has been linked to specific projects, such as Highway at Selby or the Whitby Community project, which are partnership projects between colleges, universities and community organisations.

Since the concept of the staged engagement model was first developed in 2007/8, reflection and revisions have influenced how it has been delivered and to whom. Colleges have used it strategically to support the following policies, plans or developments:

- Priorities in their higher education strategy
- Widening participation strategic assessment
- Utilisation of resources that had been made available in local communities, such as the Green Lane Centre in Whitby
- Local area regeneration strategies
- Focus of local economic development, such as creative media industry in Scarborough
- Meeting particular skill shortage or developing markets
- Increased internal progression and retention rates
- Increased partnership working
- Identifying areas of curriculum for future development, so that students had appropriate pathways from Level 3 provision
- Testing the market for the future potential of specific foundation degrees or market demand
- Supporting progression for new sectors of students, such as those from ethnic minority groups.

While many colleges felt that the time spent on marketing, development and delivery compared with the actual income – and often the outcome – meant that the model was not really a viable one, they all wanted to continue with the staged engagement model, because it supported so many of their priorities. There might be other opportunities in the future to look at different models, such as fully funded modules.

One college discussed with HEFCE the strategic advantage of being able to have their own directly funded 'bite-size' ASNs, but the administrative burden it would place on HEFCE means it is unlikely to happen in the near future.

From discussions with partners it is clear that the staged engagement model has provided a range of indirect benefits which can be enhanced by future developments. The benefits include:

- Increased skills and confidence reported by learners

- More joint working between HE and FE staff

- Development of further links with HEIs, especially in the area of research

- Delivery of joint CPD with HEIs

- Support for Aimhigher work and agendas

- Development of external progression agreements

- Ability to explore future applications, such as embedding a Level 4 module into diplomas

- Identification of challenges that students face progressing from vocational qualifications

- The potential for bite-size delivery as an additional offering to HE provision

- Enabling colleges to operate more responsively to recruitment trends and community/employer needs

- Allowing colleges to pilot certain provision.

Partner colleges used a range of different marketing approaches and these were linked to the target audience. Colleges which used staged engagement to attract external students used a much wider range of marketing routes than the colleges who were using it as a more internal progression or retention tool.

These approaches included:

- Part-time prospectus

- Newspaper adverts

- Website

- Mail shots direct to employers/learners

- Flyers in libraries

- Dedicated brochures

- Use of internal CRM system

- Next Steps and other delivery partners

- Postcards

- Word of mouth.

Colleges also commented that the time of year that ASNs were allocated affected their marketing strategies. Prospectuses were often produced before ASNs were allocated, so they missed an ideal marketing opportunity.

Community models, which involved multiple partners in a semi-rural area, such as Selby, or where the ethos of learning was not embedded into the community, needed different marketing strategies. Evaluation of the Selby project suggested that using existing networks and local community workers would have been the most effective way of engaging with local people and community groups. These could include Health Visitors, Family Learning Tutors or Sure Start staff who should have a part to play in a wider college strategy regarding progression from lower level qualifications through to level 4. But learners in a community-based model often need additional support and take-up can be affected by who delivers the course – and where – and by more practical arrangements such as the availability of childcare.

Where colleges used staged engagement for internal progression or to support retention, for example, through the delivery of study skills models, the marketing costs were generally lower, but this was offset by the amount of time staff used on promoting courses internally or liaising with other FE staff or other colleges in the area. Staff also had to commit time to reminding people about attendance.

One of the best marketing tools seemed to be the actual course itself. If the module was aimed at a skill need in the local area, or filled a need for a particular employer or supported a specific progression need, such as Algebra for Engineers, the numbers attending were healthy. One of the colleges, which had recently undertaken some research with employers in the local areas, felt that their offer of bite-size modules would have looked a lot different if they had had the outcomes of the research earlier. Niche marketing was used by some of the colleges where they had very specific industries or client groups, but this relied very much on the tutor's prior knowledge of local industry and well-developed links with these employers. Also some of the feedback from colleges and projects indicated that courses that offered a wider breadth of learning and had more general appeal – such as creative writing and health and society – attracted more learners.

Some college staff felt that take-up was affected by the time of day at which modules were delivered. Some colleges felt that the take-up was low because modules were run through the day, but were aimed more at people who were at work and that modules marketed as a twilight session might have had more take-up. There was a need to explore delivery on Saturdays. Furthermore, although some colleges wanted to run study skills modules in early September, ASNs have to be used by July, which again affects the way in which modules can be marketed.

Organisation and lead-in times for the programmes also affected take-up, sometimes leading to increased numbers of 'targeted' learners or learners in particular curriculum areas. This also seemed to have led to increased progression.

With some colleges there was a real difference in the take-up of ASNs between 2007/8 and 2008/9. This reduction in numbers could not be entirely attributed to the marketing of the bite-size provision – take-up is often influenced by what the market wants at that particular time and the circumstances relating to that market. However, the use of expert sessions was a good marketing tool, since it allowed colleges, for example, to bring in well-known experts from a particular industry or use the funding to do something in a very creative way, such as using a theatre group to work with potential education and childcare students.

One college felt tutors themselves could make a greater contribution to marketing staged engagement. There was a need to increase awareness of the staged engagement model as a progression and retention tool, which would allow learners to 'try before they buy'. Several colleges said that staged engagement was just as useful for learners who subsequently decided that HE was not for them at this particular time, as it was for learners who decided to progress.

The discussion showed that no one marketing strategy worked and that it very much depended on the local area, the type of students or potential learners that were being targeted, as well as the module that was on offer. It also provided some surprises – modules that colleges thought would go really well did not attract numbers, where others attracted large numbers with the Whitby project maintaining a waiting list for one of their modules. With the Highway project in Selby the Creative Writing module run by the Centre of Lifelong Learning at the University of York, which was part of the project, attracted a very diverse range of learners quite different from the usual client group that they attracted in York. The social make-up of the geographical area clearly had some influence on the take-up and the success of the marketing campaigns or methods. Colleges also pointed to the importance of the company profile in the area and colleges with a larger percentage of SMEs in the area found it hard to attract employer sponsored learners.

The flexibility of the staged engagement model and the fact that it could be adapted to the local area's needs, the colleges' priorities and learner demands was one of the successes of the model[1].

Judging by the number of applications for YHELLN support for staged engagement projects, the ethos behind the staged engagement model has been embraced by the YHELLN partners. Inevitably, not all expert

---

1   For further details of the YHELLN experience with staged engagement see *All the Best: Staged Engagement, YHELLN Good Practice Guide*, 2009.

sessions could be funded. In general, the applications that did not receive funding were not in the YHELLN curriculum areas. Admittedly, the model was introduced to partners after the traditional timetabling had been set in many institutions, and so a number did not have the internal capacity to adopt the model straight away. This could be rectified for future curriculum planning.

The question of whether staged engagement is reaching the target audience of employers and non-traditional learners is still open for discussion. Future development should be more precisely targeted to attract potential learners who more closely fit the needs of the wider business community. Indeed, the staged engagement model has proved to be a positive and effective tool in the engagement of employers and learners, when it is precisely targeted and appropriate to the learner needs and values. Lessons have been learnt for the future planning of expert session and bite-size modules, with partners becoming increasingly aware of the strategic significance of staged engagement as a useful and pragmatic tool for employer engagement and widening participation in higher education.

If the Leitch target and HE skills at work are to be met, then the challenge is now on for HE providers to devise workforce development practices and initiatives. With reference to knowledge exchange and brokerage, HE providers must realise that learning and development is a two-way process; practice informing theory and theory informing practice. No-one should assume that educational providers are the sole keepers and disseminators of knowledge. Barnett (1999) suggests:

> The more radical step in collective understanding – that we can all learn from each other- is much more rarely taken on board. And it is partly the existential challenges to one's personal authority, status and legitimacy that the further step would usher in that prevents it from being seriously tackled.

Higher Education has a potentially crucial role to play in supporting employers and organisations to remain effective and competitive through knowledge exchange and as knowledge brokers. Therefore, the UK does not simply require more graduates, it needs those who have the knowledge, skills and competencies to contribute positively to the growth of the economy, and who can enhance the knowledge exchange base that has been laid down by many educational institutions.

CHAPTER FOUR

Progression and Progression Agreements

Charlie Sanders

The Leitch Review of Skills published in 2006 foresaw the need to improve the level of skill of the populace as 'the key lever' for generating increased employment, productivity, prosperity and social justice. It called for the UK to commit to being a world leader in skills by 2020, an ambition that would require a doubling of attainment at most levels of skill. To achieve such a demanding target – and to do so in a context where the number of young people in the population will continue to fall until around 2025 – would require major efforts on behalf of government, employers and individuals themselves. Central government set a number of targets, significantly calling for 40% of the population to achieve higher education qualifications by 2020.

In this context, YHELLN sought in particular to focus on increasing progression opportunities for those who had achieved their Level 3 qualifications via a vocational route. YHELLN immediately recognised, however, that its local geographical area would strongly influence the nature of progression that could be achieved. Serving an area bounded by Whitby, Grimsby and Doncaster at its points, the area is rural with infrequent bus services and poor transport infrastructure. The LLN area contained only one HEI in the University of Hull. Distances can be substantial. The area, covering approximately 2,500 square miles, stretches 65 miles from north to south and 50 miles at its maximum east to west extent. Transport routes are in many cases dictated by costs. These are inflated where there is a need to cross the Humber Bridge, a major unifying geographic feature which in other socio-economic ways divides the YHELLN area. YHELLN realised that because of the nature of the area the model of FE centres feeding into one HEI was never going to be sufficient on its own. It would have to sit alongside more local progression arrangements, where Level 3 students progressed to HE courses either in their own FE institution or in a neighbouring one.

Following the start of YHELLN in January 2007 the Directorate, along with the Steering Group, developed their aims in the area of progression as follows:

> The role of Lifelong Learning Networks.........includes putting in place a range of measures to ensure that vocational learners are able to access, succeed in and progress through higher education opportunities that meet their needs. Progression agreements are a vital tool in creating and sustaining the necessary changes in order to provide these opportunities, and sit alongside other aspects of LLN work such as mechanisms for credit accumulation and transfer, increasing the flexibility (content and mode) of the curriculum offer and ensuring appropriate advice and guidance is available.

The working definition of a progression agreement is: 'a formal statement of entitlement to enter a programme of study made specific to an individual or small, defined group of learners'.

This was adopted internally to the Network in order to facilitate understanding between all internal stakeholders. The phrase 'guaranteed progression' was avoided as it is misleading and may cause unnecessary concern.

The appointment of a Progression Manager to develop work around the area of Progression agreements and other progression issues was made later in 2007.

YHELLN's strategic response to the challenge of increasing progression included:

- Fostering the creation of formalised progression agreements within and between institutions
- The development of a range of activities designed to raise progression opportunities and aspiration across the network

- Encouraging a range of learner support measures designed to market and promote opportunities in HE.

In its original Business Plan YHELLN envisaged four major work strands, namely:

- Progression agreements/ Curriculum developments (content and mode)

- Learner support, learner portfolios, entitlement (including Lifelong)

- Research, evaluation and professional development

- Communications (including IAG, Agency Liaison [Aimhigher, Sector Skills,

- Regional Skills, Employers])

YHELLN's emphasis throughout has been on vocational learners and the need to ensure improved opportunities in HE. Aims from its original business plan relevant to progression were seen as:

- Sustaining, facilitating and increasing access routes to HE, with particular emphasis on vocational pathways needed for local students.

- Many of the target learners will be those already engaged on a progression pathway but who would benefit from further choice in moving forward.

- YHELLN's progression agreements will in part focus on the challenge of opening up more opportunities for existing learners

- YHELLN would seek to underpin all its offers of progression with an uncomplicated and assured framework for progression based on clear and guaranteed guidelines, such as the model adopted by the Canadian College system in Manitoba.

The business plan stated very clearly: 'We do not underestimate the task of achieving this aim and of sustaining the guarantee that lies at its heart, whether it is a matter of transfer between programmes or between institutions. There is a particular responsibility that lies with the HEIs as awarding bodies to make sure that the progression agreements are honoured and sustained over time'.

Further, the plan stated that: 'without such a progression framework in place, the confidence that 14–19 learners and older learners can place in vocational choices will not equal that felt by more traditional, academic learners. YHELLN will give that confidence, offering security as well as an entitlement to flexibility. The defining of the parameters of flexibility will be one of the most important challenges for YHELLN'.

So, what are the principles of progression that YHELLN adopted in developing its strategy?

Progression is a term widely used in education and elsewhere, and with a wide number of meanings. In the context of YHELLN, progression was used in ensuring that an individual was able to move to the next appropriate level in their chosen area of vocational study. In some circumstances it was clear that curricular deficiencies meant that a particular institution might offer Level 2 and Level 4 in specific subject areas, whilst a Level 3 course was unavailable. A student on this chosen subject route would, therefore, be unable to progress within that particular institution. In order to progress a student might have to go elsewhere, i.e. follow a different progression route for purposes of study.

The concept of a 'progression agreement' was seen as a way of ensuring that an individual student would be able to move up from one institution to another carrying credit with them as they moved up the levels of attainment e.g. from Level 3 to Level 4 to Level 5 to Level 6. Progression agreements were not seen as necessary within an individual institution, as progression routes should exist there already; however, it was envisaged that formal progression agreements *would* be needed, if students were to move *between* institutions as they changed levels.

The initial vision of HEFCE was that progression agreements would be made between a pre-cursor and a receiving institution and that a guarantee of a place would be made between them. It was envisaged that Lifelong Learning Networks would broker agreements between institutions and soon a network of credit-bearing progression agreements would be in place across any particular LLN partnership. As in many other cases, however, the reality turned out to be different from the theory and from HEFCE's original vision.

The task of setting up progression agreements across the YHELLN partnership fell to the Progression Manager. An initial desk survey lasting approximately three months and visits across England showed that other LLNs were adopting a variety of methods in relation to progression agreements. Discussion with colleagues revealed that in some LLNs progression agreement credit frameworks had been established covering all areas of the curriculum, in all institutions involved, with routes and signposting provided through web-based portals. Other LLNs used passport-type certificates issued to all vocational students who wished to progress offering a variety of guarantees including: guaranteed numbers of ring-fenced places, guaranteed places without limit, guaranteed offers of a place or guaranteed interviews. Some LLNs were covering curriculum at all levels from 3–8, others were concentrating mainly on vocational Level 3–4. There was apparently no set pattern and no set model. It became clear, therefore, that YHELLN would need to take in elements of good practice from various areas but in essence would need to develop its own model for progression.

At the same time as the initial desk survey was being undertaken, a Progression Working Group was established. Representatives from each of the YHELLN partners plus two of the Higher Skills Team Leaders came together in late 2007 to form the Working Group under the chairmanship of the Progression Manager. The group considered progression issues from first principles and developed a framework for progression agreements that would be workable and acceptable for all member institutions of the partnership.

This framework gradually developed during the next nine months, so that by July 2008 we were able to launch the YHELLN Progression Toolkit. The toolkit contained a wide range of advice and materials about producing progression agreements and included a pro forma 'programme progression agreement' that would be used for the production of all YHELLN progression agreements. Once launched, the toolkit went into operation and very soon one of our partner colleges had developed progression agreements with two other institutions, interestingly from outside of our LLN area. (Latterly, the YHELLN Toolkit model was adopted by various other LLNs).

In order to ensure acceptance of the Progression Toolkit and its contents and building on the YHELLN Strategic Statement on Progression Agreements of some 12 months earlier, the Progression Manager produced a 'YHELLN Accord on Progression Agreements', reiterating the background and philosophy of progression agreements as developed by YHELLN. The Accord, including an agreement to develop and embed progression agreements across the network, was duly accepted and signed by authorised senior management team representatives of the YHELLN partnership in June 2008.

The principles of progression inherent within the accord were:

- Some learners will be enthusiastic about progressing to a full qualification which may take two or three years to complete; others will find it suits them better to advance in smaller stages, such as 'bite-size' provision or a university foundation module.

- Progression agreements and other strategies to support progression would not promise, or appear to promise, more than can actually be guaranteed.

- All progression arrangements would require clear, unambiguous support from senior management levels in the relevant institutions.

- Progression arrangements must be underpinned by effective guidance for learners. Guidance assumes increasing importance as learners progress, both in the short and longer term.

- Both formal and informal progression arrangements have clear benefits for the 'receiving' institution or programme, but must also recognise that learners have a choice about institutions they wish to attend or programmes they wish to pursue.

- Mechanisms must be in place to ensure that the receiving institution – or programme – is aware that a student has arrived wholly or substantially because a progression agreement is in place.

The process for creating a progression agreement is described fully in the Progression Agreement Toolkit which advised that:

The impetus for creating a progression agreement may arise in a number of ways, but must always be beneficial both to the students and the institutions involved. YHELLN is especially concerned that they should increase opportunities for vocational learners.

A progression agreement needs to consider the content, learning outcomes and levels of achievement from both the 'pre-cursor' and 'receiving' courses. These must be carefully mapped to ensure full compatibility between the two (or more) courses, paying particular attention to the position of learners who switch specialism. Experience suggests that the mapping process should concentrate initially on areas where significant numbers of students could decide to change courses.

Where the mapping process identifies gaps in a learner's experience, some remedial input has to be arranged to fill in the missing knowledge or experience. In practice, the receiving institution will normally find ways of doing this, although on occasion it could be necessary to advise attendance at a suitable evening class.

Following mapping, it is particularly important to consider exactly what offer can be made and the nature of any conditions which may apply. The offer may be of a place or of an interview, although a place may not necessarily be available in the current year and may be subject to conditions, such as achievement of specified levels of attainment or completion of certain modules.

Institutions should consider what documentation is appropriate. The Toolkit offers a range of suitable forms together with guidance on their completion. Many of these forms are optional, the exception being the Programme Progression Agreement which identifies specific vocational progression routes between two or more partner institutions.

Progression agreements should be reviewed regularly to ensure continuing validity, and account be taken of any changes – for example, in curriculum – in either the precursor or receiving programme.

In implementing progression agreements across the partnership, it soon became clear that various factors, including the inherent features of the partnership, the partner institutions themselves and the geographic spread and nature of the YHELLN area, were starting to create problems that had not been foreseen. The geographic nature of the YHELLN area has already been noted. The dispersed nature of the urban areas spread widely across 2,500 square miles, with poor and expensive transport in the intervening rural areas, plus the intrusive nature of the Humber estuary whose banks are connected by means of a toll bridge, meant that large movement by students between centres was limited and unlikely.

Furthermore, with only one HEI within the YHELLN region, local FE colleges in the urban centres have in many cases developed a large portfolio of HE programmes through various validation and franchise arrangements over the past 15 years. Several of the validating partner institutions are from outside of the Humber area and are not YHELLN partners. As a consequence, these traditionally 'FE only' colleges are now providing their own urban centres with a high level of both FE and HE provision at the same institution and sometimes on the same site. A central tenet of several of these institutions during their development into FE/HE hybrid providers has been that many of their students will progress from FE to HE within that institution. It is axiomatic in the case of many non-traditional students in these centres that the HE experience means attending their local FE college. Financial, time, personal, employment, family and other commitments mean that, in reality, they will follow an HE programme only in their local area. It became clear that if HE provision was not available locally, students would not take part in HE at all! Given the Leitch agenda with its emphasis on the upskilling of the workforce, often in a local and work-based context, it appeared that the concept of inter-institutional progression agreements was not perhaps the most appropriate approach for some partners in the YHELLN area in answering this call.

What did become apparent, as discussion about progression agreements continued, was that several of the larger FE colleges with a high level of HE provision were concerned about their internal progression – that is those students who would complete an FE programme at their college, but would not then progress onto an HE programme with them. In some cases, facilitating internal progression was seen as a greater challenge than inter-institutional progression into other YHELLN partners.

On a slightly different scale, it is worthy of note that during 2008, discussions and informal meetings with colleagues responsible for progression agreements and issues in other LLNs in the Yorkshire area resulted in the development of the Greater Yorkshire Progression Group. This included colleagues from South Yorkshire, West Yorkshire,

Higher York, Yorkshire and Humber East, Nottinghamshire and Derby, VETNET and Lancashire Lifelong Learning Networks. The group met at regular intervals during the last 18 months and became a forum for the discussion of progression issues.

In order to overcome the various problems that had been identified during its first year or so, YHELLN latterly sought to increase progression activity in four main areas, namely:

- The development of inter-institutional progression agreements

- The development of intra-institutional progression pathways

- Progression activities funded through YHELLN projects

- The production of a Progression Good Practice Guide as one of a series of such guides produced by YHELLN.

As time progressed, more of the partner institutions started to develop inter-institutional progression agreements. Various types evolved; some were made between two FE colleges, where they saw mutual benefit in students having greater opportunities to top up at Levels 5, 6 and 7 in two institutions rather than just one. Other colleges developed this type of progression agreement with the University of Hull, offering students widened progression opportunities from Levels 3, 5 and 6.

Further opportunity for the development of progression agreements came from local Diploma Consortia. As Level 3 Diplomas developed locally, it was important that these cohorts of students were assured that this new qualification allowed for their progression onto an HE programme. The use of progression agreements between the Diploma consortia and local HE providers has proved a powerful tool in confirming progression routes locally, to the satisfaction of students, parents, schools and other feeder colleges. By the time YHELLN closed, there were 44 Inter-institutional progression agreements in place, covering a wide spectrum of subject areas and levels, with more in development.

Intra-institutional progression pathways have proved popular in FE colleges that also provide HE. In some institutions, there appeared a mismatch between numbers of students completing vocational Level 3 programmes and the number of students progressing to Level 4, even after allowing for those who entered the world of work and those students who progressed on to HE or higher level professional courses elsewhere. The use of a Progression Pathway Agreement between the FE and HE parts of the college has proved useful in highlighting the range of HE opportunities that exist within an institution and for encouraging progression to HE in a wide number of vocational areas.

The use of such intra-institutional progression pathways or internal progression agreements has proved useful in maintaining momentum for students completing a Level 3 or access course. A Progression Certificate offering the promise of a place – or an interview for a place on their chosen HE course should they complete a particular level on their present FE courses – is a real fillip to many students and gives them something to aspire to. Success on their present course means that they know where they are going.

Complementing the use of both internal and external progression agreements have been a variety of YHELLN-funded projects covering a range of progression issues. Partners have developed a variety of projects aimed at improving progression rates from FE to HE. Several colleges have developed HE activity days for students to give them the opportunity to experience HE practices and/or meet with individuals already in HE. Others have involved the use of experts from various fields who started off their career as vocational FE students. Some projects have worked with cohorts of non-traditional students in developing their aspirations and getting them to consider how they might progress their lives and careers through use of the FE and HE educational systems. Others have allowed for the development of CPD opportunities for staff in relation to progression issues or allowed time for staff to develop closer ties between their curricula, so making transition between FE and HE programmes a much smoother operation.

The processes and activities listed above have all been part of the developmental process of finding ways and developing practices to improve progression opportunities for students in the YHELLN area. The final area of activity has been the drawing together of ideas and activities that demonstrate good practice in the area of progression and their publication. The development of a series of Good Practice Guides under the generic title of *All the Best* aims to show how the work developed through YHELLN can be adopted and practised by our partners and, indeed, other similar institutions. *The Good Practice Guide for Progression* includes information about the principles and practice of progression and then covers a series of case studies from local partners who have used YHELLN funding to improve the progression rates from FE to HE for their students. The guide stands as a good starting point for any FE institution wishing to improve its progression rates and is equally valuable to practitioners in HEI and HE provider institutions who are interested in looking at ways to improve recruitment locally onto their programmes.

The concept of progression is now fairly well understood in the academic world. As YHELLN progressed, it became clear that the partner institutions viewed progression for their students as an important and integral part of their work. What some of the partners did require, however, was help in developing or improving the processes involved in ensuring appropriate progression and making them more effective. All partners became involved in projects that involved progression activities, aimed at enhancing progression opportunities for their students or potential students.

The idea of progression agreements was something that took a long time to embed across the network. Some partners had developed something like this before, for example, progression compacts with local schools, but others had no experience in this area. It, therefore, took some time for the concept of progression agreements as intended by HEFCE, to become accepted by all members of the partnership, although all ultimately did and signed up to the process through the YHELLN Accord on Progression Agreements.

As time progressed, several progression agreements developed and YHELLN can claim success in this area, although it became clear at an early stage that partners were *not* prepared to enter into agreements that specifically *guaranteed a place on a programme*. Although this was the idea originally propounded by HEFCE as they set up the Lifelong Learning Networks, no HE provider in the YHELLN area was prepared to make an offer of this nature. This is due to a variety of factors. In November 2007 HEFCE effectively placed a cap on ASN numbers and the opportunities for growth through this mechanism virtually ceased. Further, the economic downturn starting in 2008 led to an increase in numbers of students attending HE, and although this may be just a temporary increase, most partners in YHELLN have recruited to target numbers and do not feel they can afford to guarantee any further individual places through the use of progression agreements. It remains to be seen whether or not the use of progression agreements will increase as student numbers in the traditional 19-year-old age group start to fall, in line with demographic changes predicted for the period 2011–20.

Although progression agreements between institutions have not proved as popular with providers as might have been predicted or desired, many other areas of progression activity have developed and been most successful. Given the fact that several of the partner colleges in YHELLN are large providers of both FE and HE provision and given the dispersed and isolated geographic distribution of their urban centres, it is not surprising that much more emphasis has been focused on the development of *internal progression pathway* arrangements, leading particularly to higher numbers of Level 3 students progressing onto HE programmes within the same institution. If these students did not move on to an HE programme in their immediate locale, they would not progress to HE at all; hence the importance of such internal progression pathway agreements.

Many partners used YHELLN project funding to develop progression-based activities that would raise students' awareness of opportunities afforded by HE with the intention of increasing the number of students progressing onto HE programmes. Such projects took many forms, such as HE Experience Away Days, extended visits to universities and other HEIs, development of summer schools, participation by students in specific university / HE provider activities, bridging programmes targeted at students from countries that have recently joined the EU, CPD events for FE staff at HEIs and progression conferences.

What became clear from this range of activities, as YHELLN moved towards its close and the outcomes from the projects were evaluated, was that the concept of *progression* – although not necessarily expressed through progression agreements – was becoming much more mainstream across the partnership than it had hitherto been. All partners realised the importance of progression for all of their students or potential students, and that clearly planned and specifically targeted progression activities were fundamental to ensuring that more of their students took the opportunity to progress on to HE.

Finally, YHELLN's progression strategy has helped develop coherence between its three specified work strands of Progression, Learner Support and IAG, and Curriculum Development. It was clear that these three work strands, each with its own Manager, would of necessity have to work in close cooperation. This has indeed been the case and much of the work of each of these work strands has coalesced with the others. In the case of some funded projects, it has been difficult to distinguish where one area of activity begins and another ceases. Some partners, for example, having developed new curricula through the staged engagement model, have included new learner support and IAG activities to support those learners taking advantage of this new curriculum opportunity. This has led to students wanting to move on to the next stage or level of learning through use of a progression pathway agreement, taking advantage of the progression opportunities available.

The concept of progression is now firmly embedded in the collective culture and practice of the YHELLN partnership. The value of ensuring progression for all individuals in a local and regional context has been realised and many activities and processes have been introduced to ensure that progression into and through HE continues to be a central part of the work of all of the YHELLN partner institutions.

CHAPTER FIVE

Learner Support

Jane Barker

It is important to find a definition of Learner Support that clearly and concisely explains what it is. If we look at the two words separately they are defined as:

> Learn – 'to gain by experience, example, etc to become informed'

> Support – 'to give aid or courage to'

From this we can deduce that a learner receiving support could, therefore, be interpreted as being 'someone who receives encouragement and/or aid in order to gain knowledge so that they are better informed and more experienced'. It is, however, very difficult to find an overall definition or example, which covers the generic concept of learner support.

The definition below interprets learner support as:

> Additional learning support (ALS) is any activity that provides direct support for learning to individual learners, over and above that which is normally provided in a standard learning programme that leads to their learning goal.[1]

An alternative definition is more personal to the learner, who is seen in the context of an education sector which is the service provider, helping the learner to achieve.

> Learner support addresses learners' needs and empowers them to create learning experiences which are more personally meaningful, more relevant and more productive. Education has become a service industry and learner support is a key component of that service. (Kehrwald 2008)

According to the Learning and Skills Council, learner support is financial aid, as in its EMA (Education Maintenance Allowance), and does not relate to either of the above definitions, both of which describe learner support as personal rather than financial support. (LSC 2009)

If the term learner support can be defined very differently, we can expect that it is interpreted and implemented very differently by different organisations and institutions. One local college, for example, informs us that their learner support covers all aspects of a student's life, offering, for example, a counselling service, information, advice and guidance on finance, child care and the opportunity to have a Learning Mentor. It describes additional learning support for those who may have disabilities and help with basic skills for those who may have literacy and numeracy support needs. Other colleges have learning support, which provides the same range of services, and in addition, they have student support services delivering basic skills and disability support.

These statements are descriptions of service. They inform how a particular college views learner support and give the learner or potential learner a list of supports or services. However, they may not always tell us the college's overall aim or ethos or show what outcomes they intend from their provision of learner support. Whilst lists and clarity of what can be expected are extremely useful, they are limited if they do not include other areas of learner support, i.e. what will the learner do to get what they particularly need? But lists of this sort don't necessarily give us the full picture – we need to know, for instance, what the learner will do to get what they particularly need.

Comparing the role of learner support to those of teacher/tutor, manager, doctor or traffic warden can be useful as these roles are more generally understood. These roles have clear boundaries and people who come into contact with them usually understand the rules of engagement and what they are likely to receive. There are likely to be clear-cut and well defined reasons, which will be different for each as to why the relationship is being established in the first place and that will affect the interactions that subsequently take place.

Understanding what is on offer within titles of advertised services can help you to consider what learners' needs are and will hopefully lessen any potential disappointments if the service, or in this case, support is not delivered or offered.

Titles within the services can also be quite diverse yet describe similar or the same jobs. Learner support managers and assistants generally ensure the delivery of basic skills in literacy and numeracy. They do not necessarily have anything to do with supporting learners to access issues related to their next education or career steps or possible issues in their personal life. On the other hand, there are learner support managers who deliver a wide range of supportive systems, but nothing to do with, for example, basic skills, as this is seen as falling under the teaching remit.

In organisations outside the education establishments learner support is often closely linked to Information, Advice and Guidance (IAG). This type of service is usually linked to the delivery of what was once called Careers Advice, but with the change in approaches to education, training and work patterns, this is now more commonly called IAG. The icg workforce website (www.Icgworkforce-uk.org) describes this service as:

- Developing career-related knowledge and career exploration, management and employability skills

- Having access to accurate, up-to-date, comprehensive and objective information about all their options including 14–19 Diplomas

- Receiving impartial advice and guidance that supports career exploration, decision-making, progression planning and transition.

IAG is an important part of the learner support activity and can be seen in some descriptions of learner support as a separate entity, but one which nevertheless affects the delivery of other parts. For example, information can be offered to learners about the course they have enquired about; advice can then be given about which courses are available and why they could be of interest. Then guidance can be offered to enable the learner to consider all the effects that their intended action could make on both themselves and others.

> There is clear evidence that access to IAG increases the likelihood that individuals will enter learning and that they will achieve a qualification from their study. (Adult Guidance policy team, 2003)

As far back as 2004, John Denham, while addressing the Fabian Society, said: 'what people need are services able to support and guide them through the complex choices they have to make'. (Denham, 2004)

After that, the Leitch Review of Skills (2006) argued that the service should have significant targeted features and it should: 'be charged with raising aspiration and awareness of the importance and benefits of learning, particularly among those that have missed out in the past'.

The delivery of IAG is also an area for discussion. Is it confined only to those with a specifically relevant job title or description or is it something that a number of other professionals, for example teachers/tutors, can also deliver? Many teachers and tutors have always tried to support their students with information outside of the curriculum area they are actually teaching. This could be regarding relationships at home that are affecting the student in school – students may confide in the teacher who in turn tries to help – or it could be with regard to which university course to apply for. But there are issues here too:

- How are they qualified to do this?

- How does the recipient of the advice know that what they are being given is up-to-date and relevant?

- How do we ensure quality of delivery across all these organisations and institutions and across all the numbers of people involved in giving all or part of the possible information, advice and guidance?

At the moment there isn't anything to say that only trained professionals can deliver IAG or parts of what can be classified as IAG.

Other aspects of learner support are sometimes given different titles and can be delivered by a wide range of people. Recent initiatives have supported students' transition from one key stage to another, or progression from one course to another or indeed one institution to another, but isn't such transition support really learner support under another name? Mentoring is another significant area that should be examined, particularly as to how we select and train mentors, what we expect from them and what do the mentees themselves expect from these interventions?

All of the above are part of learner support activity. This concept of learner support suggests a definition along the following lines: 'encouragement and/or aid received by a learner in order to gain knowledge and experience about learning, so that they are better informed'.

Learner support can be found in a variety of roles and titles and delivered by professionally trained people or perhaps by those who have experience, but not necessarily professional training.

Perhaps I can best express what I mean by using the analogy of an open umbrella, where each of the spokes of the umbrella represents an aspect of this overarching concept of learner support. Understanding of the concept of learner support 'need' is the key to a more uniform interpretation of 'need'.

Firstly there needs to be a consensus of what learner support is, together with agreement and acknowledgement of who can deliver it, including those who do not necessarily carry the job title or job description. Secondly, there should also be agreement of the overarching values and ethos of learner support, which covers all organisations and institutions. Thirdly, lists of services can show what can and can't be gained. Fourthly, clarity of terminology will help sweep away diverse interpretations and applications.

Once we have approached this clarity of understanding and delivery, learner support can be acknowledged in all its glory and the grey mist of confusion as to what it actually is, can be lifted for one and all.

CHAPTER SIX

Why Understanding LMI is Important

Jane Barker with Laura Minghella

YHELLN recognised that information, advice and guidance would play a key role in achieving its mission to increase opportunities for all learners in higher education but perhaps more particularly vocational learners. One component of the information, advice and guidance process is the importance within vocational learning to provide up-to-date and accessible information about jobs in the local labour market and the learning and qualifications available in gaining employment or searching the labour market for alternative opportunities. Labour Market Information (LMI) is one key tool in offering this information to support informed decisions.

Labour Market Information has implications for making career decisions, reinforcing the need for continuing education and training and supporting strategic planning.

> When someone receives good labour market information that leads to a good decision, it benefits the individual, the employer and the economy. (DfES 2004, *LMI Matters! Understanding labour market information*)

Many of us have heard about labour market information, some of us try to use labour market information, but possibly only a few actually know what it is and how to use it effectively. There are various definitions of a labour market, which enable us to draw out key points about LMI. For example:

> The term 'labour market' is used to refer to the interactions between those in need of labour (employers or buyers) and those who can supply labour (employees or sellers). (*LMI Matters* 2007)

> Labour market information (LMI) is information about the structure
> and working of a labour market and any factors likely to influence the
> structure and working of that market. (*LMI* YNY 2009)

Information about a labour market tends to focus on who is recruiting
labour and which industries are growing and declining. The type of labour
that is being hired can be set against what sort of labour is available. This
can also be referred to as labour demand and supply. LMI usually refers
to data found in tables, spreadsheets, maps, graphs, charts, or reports
which are often from reliable and robust sources such as Annual Business
Inquiry and NOMIS, an online database Office for National Statistics.

Other sources could be newspaper articles or anecdotes, but these data
are not 'robust' because of their source. None of these data are of use
until they are interpreted.

This interpretation can aid understanding and can be used to forecast
what jobs could be available in the future and which people could be
available to do those jobs. Forecasting, therefore, is a key issue. Once it
has been analysed, the information can be referred to as labour market
intelligence.

In addition to these definitions, it is also useful to define labour demand
and labour supply in terms of a labour market.

> A labour market is a mechanism which matches potential employers
> of people – labour demand – with people who are available for work
> – labour supply. (DfES 2005, *Understanding the Labour Market*)

Labour demand is the actual need for labour in the workforce and
provides information about where the jobs are. For example, it includes
information about which industries are taking on staff and which are
shedding staff plus the type and level of occupations that are in demand.
It also shows employment in terms of work patterns, such as shift
working or part-time, temporary or casual employment, together with the
levels of skills and qualifications needed to do the jobs available.

Labour supply is the people who make up the workforce. Information on
labour supply comes from the number of people available to work – that
is the potential labour force and how it is made up. It looks at the gender
profile, ethnic mix, age and disability plus the skills and qualifications level

of the labour force. Finally, it looks at the number of unemployed people and the travel-to-work patterns of the labour force.

A labour market is usually broken down into industrial sectors and occupations and by geographical areas. The labour market is in constant change as it responds to the needs of employers, who in turn respond to influences in the wider environment, such as demographics, globalisation, education and training, technological change, government policy, exchange rates and import and export issues.

All the above makes up LMI and can, therefore, inform those who access this information about where jobs are currently located and where they might be in the future, about the current size of the sector and how it might change in coming years. Geographically it could indicate where specific jobs are more likely to be found which might not always match where living choices have been made. This raises mobility issues. It can also show the amount of competition for jobs within industry sectors and the hours and wages that can be realistically expected. Finally, it can indicate the skills and qualities employers are looking for together with entry routes into jobs, career structures training requirements and the potential areas for self-employment.

Labour market information has been seen to be of increasing importance over the past few years in the support of education, training and, ultimately, career choices and decision-making. This is supported and clarified by the National Policy Framework statement on national and local labour market information and intelligence

> This should be in a format which is accessible to the user and provides the most up-to-date and accurate information on the labour market at national, regional and local level including local employer information and trends; with career, occupational and sector profiles. (DfES 2003, *The National Policy Framework and Action Plan for IAG for adults*)

From this we can see that accuracy and currency are key points, but based on the following, so are clarity and ease of access for even the youngest user.

> 11–19 year olds do not need to know about changing employment patterns in detail, but they do need to understand general labour market

trends and how to access sources of labour market information. (DfES 2007, *Understanding the Labour Market*)

Research has shown that employment patterns have changed in recent years, from ones that saw some people having 'a job for life', to individuals who will have to adapt to career changes which could include training or retraining at various points during their working life. The urgency to do so in a recession highlights the fact that, in Heraclitus's words: 'The only constant is change'. (Heraclitus 535–454BC)

Heraclitus still has resonance today for those in a job, with employers requiring individuals who are flexible and adaptable to fill the job roles that are required today and in the future. For example, there are very few employment opportunities nowadays for 'fence viewers or knocker-ups'. There is, however, a growth in the creative and media industries, for example, as the entertainment industry booms, as well as in repair services as ageing populations can no longer do the household DIY tasks.

It is clear that in order for those seeking to change their jobs and future employees to be able to make informed decisions, they will require access to enhanced careers guidance that includes LMI. The ability to access this remotely in the current technological age is invaluable.

Knowledge of labour market trends and how to access labour market information is important at whatever stage individuals plan to enter the labour market. It is also important for those who offer education, training, advice and guidance to access and understand the needs or potential needs of employers in order that the 'offer ' they make is relevant and up to date. For example, in the case of education institutions, they need to offer courses to equip students with relevant knowledge for the future work place. They also need to ensure accurate and up-to-date information is available for those offering advice and guidance to their clients.

Much of the current LMI points towards 'continuous and faster' change in the workplace and shows that the importance of higher level skills will continue to rise as well, should individuals wish to progress in their chosen career. They are more likely to make realistic personal plans to maximise their employment opportunities if they accept these changes and, by understanding the labour market, the relevance of continuous education or lifelong learning will be clear and acceptable. It should also give an individual ownership of their career planning and, therefore, assist in the planning for periods of change, retraining, or unemployment. This will have implications for their financial and other personal plans.

LMI can support both the individual and the practitioner in both short and long term career planning. Initially, the information can highlight current areas of employment growth and availability. In the longer term it can indicate areas of employment and/or specific jobs, which are in decline. An employer will not offer jobs which are no longer required. LMI will also, however, indicate employment areas of potential growth and the changes in working practices. The structure of industry and, therefore, occupations is now constantly changing which can affect opportunities and working conditions and life styles that go with them.

It has been emphasised in a number of influential documents that high quality information that can affect individual education, training and /or employment decisions, is crucial.

Leitch said as far back as 2005:

> Information failure occurs when the information available to the individuals and firms is incomplete or not good enough, or when some have more or different information to others. (Leitch, S., 2005, *Skills in the UK: the long term challenge*, London: HM Treasury)

Labour market information that can be used effectively must be accessible, user friendly, relevant and up to date, as well as robust with regard to the data content. However, unless it is understood by those who access it either as individuals, or in a professional capacity, it will not have the impact or value that it should have. As noted at the beginning:

> When someone receives good labour market information that leads to a good decision, it benefits the individual, the employer and the economy. (DfES 2004, *LMI Matters! Understanding labour market information*)

Recognising the importance of LMI, YHELLN worked with education and career partners from across York and North Yorkshire to develop a new interactive online resource designed to help students and advisers find out a lot more about learning, training and the make-up of the labour market in the area. Yorkshire and Humber East Lifelong Learning

Network (YHELLN) was supported during its production by North Yorkshire Business Education Partnership (NYBEP) with the funding for the development being made available from Connexions York and North Yorkshire and YHELLN. The service was launched at the end of July 2009. More details can be found in the YHELLN series of *All the Best* guides.

The LMI York and North Yorkshire website (www.lmiyny.co.uk) provides up-to-date LMI and clear facts and figures about the area, including key companies, learning and training opportunities, transport, employment trends and industry sectors. The new website aims to make labour market information in York and North Yorkshire (LMI YNY) accessible for all in an easily understood and user-friendly way. The information presented follows national standards whilst ensuring a substantial level of local detail, which should give confidence and value to all who use it. It proves, therefore, that LMI can be an informative and useful tool for all to access.

CHAPTER SEVEN

Working with Business

Sarah Gribbin

Although employer engagement and working with employers is, or should be, implicit in vocational learning, originally it was not expressly articulated as being a work stream within YHELLN. However, the combination of starting the project and the increasing numbers of policy initiatives in this area soon brought to our attention the need to define this as a specified area of work. This not only helped to ensure that employers were identified *explicitly* as essential stakeholders in this area of work, but also helped to provide us with a focus around which to develop strategy and share experience. Thus, as the months progressed in YHELLN's work, 'working with business' became a theme around which we developed a number of conferences and staff development events, as well as sharing our experiences across our key sectors.

One of the essential aspects of YHELLN's work in increasing opportunities for vocational learners has been the element of partnership working. This involves bringing a sometimes wide variety of stakeholders together with a common purpose to achieve something that they could not as easily or effectively do individually. One manifestation of partnership working we have been involved with is that of the creation and development of sector-based groups. As we got more involved in this activity we did some research and evaluation into one of the sector groups. One of the things that became apparent was that educational partners involved in the development of the group did not appear to have a formal process for the approval of the activity nor for the authorisation of commitment of resources dedicated to support the activity. (This is not to suggest that the organisations concerned did not know what was happening, just that they did not have a standard, routine approval process that mirrored the principles of course or centre approval.)

Whilst this sort of broad-based employer engagement remained on the periphery of higher education, it was perhaps 'easier' to approve the commitment of effort and resource in this activity on a case-by-case basis as a 'one-off'. However, as the quantity of employer engagement activity grows and staff in academic institutions are encouraged to spend more of their time working with employers and in broad-based partnerships, the need for transparent, supportive and appropriate risk management and approval processes will increase and become a necessity. It is important that this activity not only fits within the overall strategy of the institution and department, but it must also be resourced and managed appropriately. This is important to YHELLN partners to help them ensure that they can take informed decisions about the activity, its strategic fit and its likely resource implications for their own institution. The development of such processes would enable senior management confidently to delegate approval of this activity to the appropriate level in the certainty that there were sound and robust systems in place.

This chapter is a product of some research carried out involving educational providers and employers relating to their involvement in sector-based groups who have come together to meet a number of objectives, some around training and education, but also including awareness raising and networking. The work explored the motivation and expectations of both the educational providers and the employers involved.

It became clear that although the motivation and expectations of the employers did combine both business and altruistic reasons, it would, however, be the business aspects that would have to show a return within a reasonable period of time. Whilst business was relatively clear about the need for a defined period of time within which the work would need to show bottom line benefits, the educational providers were far more ambiguous in their expectations in terms of articulating outcomes and time scales. This seemed to be reflected in, or a result of, the absence of internal procedures and processes for the approval and management of this kind of third-stream activity. If the process of approval for this kind of activity is compared to those developed for the approval and management of course development or approval of academic partners, it is obvious that these latter activities are far better supported. This chapter argues that:

- Most of the forms of third-stream activity currently directed at businesses has the objective of creating income streams (and hopefully profit) and, therefore, when HEIs are engaged in it, it is 'business', just as much as it is for the commercial organisations they are involved with.

- Although there is a continuum in terms of a time scale as to how immediately income generating any employer engagement activity must be, all business/employer-facing activity, be it Knowledge Exchange, Work Based Learning or involvement in broader employer engagement activity, must ultimately be able to cover its costs and hence should be viewed as 'business'. Even if activities are temporarily subsidised through initiatives such as HEIF or ECIF, they are embarked upon with a view to them at least covering costs and ideally making a contribution to 'profit'.

- Accepting the broad thrust of this argument means that HEIs involved in any of these employer engagement activities must manage these activities as a 'business' and adopt or develop appropriate strategies by which to manage the relationship.

- In management speak, this chapter defines these relationships as being 'strategic alliances' and, drawing from strategic management theory, examines what constitutes a successful strategic alliance and what needs to be done to ensure these alliances are successful for both parties.

- This argument can perhaps be relatively easily accepted using examples of Work Based Learning and Knowledge Transfer Partnerships where service levels and products can be clearly defined. For the wider ranging partnership group that can have objectives including non-financial or service delivery ones it is more complex. However, the implications in terms of reputation, resources and risk need to be equally managed. This chapter explores some of the issues that this form of employer engagement implies.

- The interviewees and the information gathered have been from those actually involved in the project. It could be that the information gathered from the interviews does not actually reflect what, on paper, their organisations may consider they already have in place. However, it does reflect the experience of those involved.

The messages coming from the case study research seem to show several themes; firstly, (and at the risk of stating the obvious) the success of employer engagement rests on the willingness of employers. Employers also need to know what is in it for them. Secondly, there is a difference in emphasis of motivations between the HEIs and the employers, the former having a broader range of motivations (perhaps fulfilling funding criteria for regional and employer engagement) and the latter a stronger emphasis on purely commercial considerations (there must be some bottom-line or strategic advantage for them). Consequently, if these forms of employer engagement are to be successful, the educational institution must have a clear strategy that it can employ so that it can develop as clear an understanding of their own motivations as do the businesses involved, and know what it is they need to do to ensure that they manage the employer engagement activity effectively.

It is, therefore, important to the HEIs to have a clear framework which they can employ that helps to define which form of employer engagement any individual activity falls into; is it full cost or does it require subsidy and does it fit with current strategy?

Such a framework must recognise the different motivations of each partner and what the implications of those are. This means, firstly, looking at the strategic fit of this sort of activity and, secondly, understanding and managing the different perspectives the organisations will draw from stakeholder management theory. Thirdly, even when the activity is partially subsidised, it must still feel and act like a professional activity to the businesses involved. Thus, the HEI should define and manage the relationship as a commercial/professional strategic alliance rather than treating it as a minor, non-core activity.

As Wedgewood's work (2007) argues, there is a broad range of expectations involved in 'employer engagement', as far as HEIs are concerned. For each of these there will be a unique set of circumstances relating to original impetus that will influence the motivation of all parties involved. Is it:

- a purely commercial provision of some 'off the shelf' training programme

- the development of a bespoke award that the HEI may also use elsewhere

- involvement in applied research

- looking to provide placements and projects for current students

- asking employers to influence strategy or curriculum development

- being involved in a sector based group that has a regional/national agenda?

There is a vast range of possible activities, but key findings of the YHELLN research included the importance of whom the activity is with, the motivation for the activity and the source of its funding. It is important to examine not just whether the activity is intended to be a commercial one; it is equally important to consider where the funding is coming from for all parties to enable them to participate, because this will help to highlight the key motivators for each activity and, hence, help develop a strategy for the successful management of it. As Gallacher (2005) argues, the success of many partnerships is limited because of different priorities and agendas that businesses and HEIs have.

Both parties may assume that the other understands them, when actually the difference between the more commercial approach taken by businesses and the cultural norms of an HEI, providing a less overtly commercial approach, can be significant. From the perspective of the employers the research highlighted the importance of there being a mutual benefit for participating in this partnership, for, although they recognised the greater good this sort of sector group may bring, having a bottom-line return was an essential element. The opportunity cost of participating in this partnership had to be clearly understood.

For businesses the source of funding for this sort of activity is their own bottom line. For HEIs the funding for working with business is often mixed and can, to some extent, be hidden in other operating costs. One HEI commented:

> (this type of sector engagement can be).... maintained by the informal route, largely because it is containable within the department – use of accommodation and amenities and informal use of staff. These costs can all be offset with a small element of contract use and, therefore, become income generating.

If the activity might have broader implications for either the department/ faculty (perhaps impacting on 'core activity') or for the wider institution, then a more formal process of discussion, consultation and approval will eventually take place, as it would with any major initiative that required resources to support it.

It is clear that at least at a departmental level, at the beginning of most types of engagement with businesses the activity takes place on an informal basis with more formal internal assessment often only taking place as and when significant resource/profile commitment is required. This form of strategy development fits well with the school of emergent strategy development and can fit well with the culture of HEIs. However, when working with commercial organisations it is also important to recognise the potential impact that the HEI's almost informal engagement may have in terms of the longer term development of the relationship.

The strategic importance being placed on 'employer engagement' by everyone from central government downwards means that the importance of successful employer engagement activity is vital. Also, the long-term relationships with commercial organisations and the ability to meet wider aspirations to make third-stream activity at least pay its own way must be considered at the very early stages of this sort of work. As has been previously stated, HEIF funding for third-stream activities is not intended to subsidise work with commercial organisations and neither is core HE funding intended to subsidise this activity. Thus, whilst still wanting to encourage these sorts of activities, it is important that the educational establishment enters into this sort of activity in as professional and business-like a manner as possible.

It might be useful if a model could be applied, capturing both the motivation for the activity and its funding source. Thus, on one axis the motivation for the activity would range from purely financial at one end to purely philanthropic at the other. The other axis would capture the source of funding ranging from purely commercial full cost activity to fully funded activity funded either through core funding or clearly identified other sources, such as central or regional funding bodies.

Hence all the activities previously mentioned can be mapped accordingly:

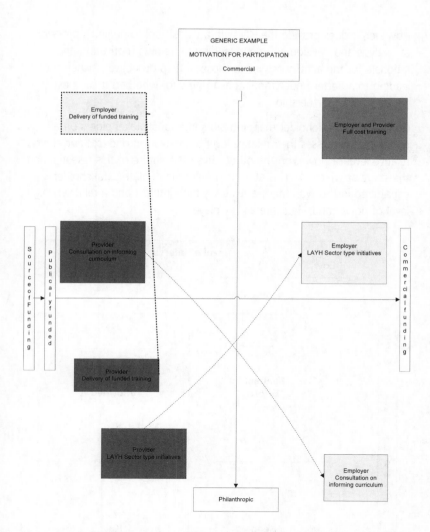

The examples used above are only indicative and assumptions have been made as to the relative level of motivation. Nevertheless, they make a useful visual representation of motivations for participation in these sorts of activities. This sort of mapping is not static and any individual initiative may move its position as a result of government policy or funding or the nature of the organisation involved (is it a charity, public sector or commercial business?).

However, it does provide the HEI with a useful tool to begin its process of analysis and develop an understanding of its own motivation and rationale for the activity as well as those of its prospective partner, thus leading to a better understanding as to how (or whether) it can best engage in the partnership.

Conventional stakeholder mapping plots individual stakeholders on a matrix that expresses their relative level of interest on one axis and their relative level of power on the other. Given the nature of this research and the stage at which LAYH is at in its development, all the stakeholders considered in this work have a relatively high interest and a relatively high level of power and, thus, are all key players.

| | Level of Interest | |
	Low	High
Low Power	Minimal Effort	Keep Informed
High Power	Keep Satisfied	Key Players

Johnson, Scholes and Whittinton, Exploring Corporate Strategy

However, applying the Motivation for Participation model, all partners can be mapped on the framework to show their relative positions.

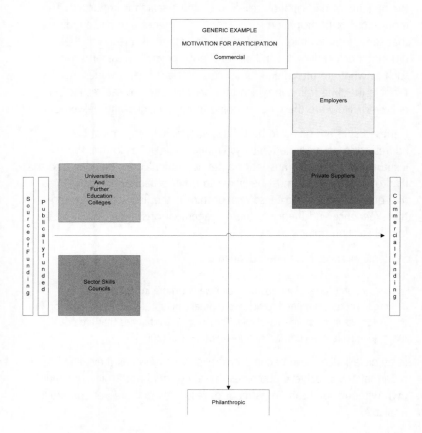

This sort of mapping exercise can reveal several things; firstly, it will show the closeness or divergence of each partner in terms of how they define the activity; secondly, each of the different quadrants indicates a different sort of relationship and/or expectations that can help inform the type/ style of approach adopted.

For most of the groups it has been applied to, it reveals the relative distance between the parties in terms of the source of funding, which allows their participation. This is especially crucial at times of economic downturn, when the pressure on commercial organisations to control costs and remain profitable is strong. Thus, the need clearly to articulate the benefits of participation revealed by the research is important. The motivation for participation shows some divergence and could indicate that some tensions might develop at some stage as a result of these differing perspectives. It can help to expose possible areas of tension, such as what are the criteria for success that each party values most? What is the time frame in which they are expecting to see results being delivered? How are these issues going to be managed and delivered?

If these issues are going to be tackled successfully, they must be addressed in an organised and systematic manner. To do this, the institutions concerned must have a defined rationale for entering into this kind of activity and it must be linked to other organisational structures and processes. Defining these relationships is the first step and using the experience and theory of the management of strategic alliances is a logical starting point.

Strategic alliances have been defined as;

> ...co-operative relationships between two or more independent organisations, designed to achieve mutually beneficial business goals for as long as is economically viable. They carry uncertainties that are not manageable in a contractual agreement. Parise (2002)

Strategic alliances have become increasingly common as they allow organisations to achieve outcomes that they could not achieve on their own without significant investment or resources that are not currently available.

Whilst there can be many motivations for entering into an alliance, Johnson, Scholes and Whittington (2005) group them into three main categories;

- Critical mass – to be achieved by bringing together partnerships of competitors or providers of complementary products to be able to deliver a better offering to the customer. This could be done through either cost reduction or by new products.

- Co-specialisation – allows the partners to bring their own specialist knowledge to the partnership and collectively create value through the synergies of the partnership. This could be through the opening up of new geographical markets or bringing different elements of the supply chain together to work more effectively.

- Learning – to gain knowledge from partners and developing skills and expertise.

They also categorise the three different forms of relationship that could constitute an alliance. The three forms all suit particular markets, require different levels of resource and suit different sorts of expectations. They are:

- Loose or market relationships in the form of networks and opportunistic alliances

- Contractual relationships in the form of licensing, franchising or subcontracting

- Ownership in the form of consortia or joint ventures.

Whichever category of alliance it is, Johnson, Scholes and Whittington also identify four key criteria for successful alliances:

- Clear strategic purpose with senior management support

- Compatibility at the operational level

- A clear definition of and an achievement of performance expectations

- Trust.

In a purely commercial setting, alliances can often be larger and more complex in nature than those described in the case study, however, in essence, the forces that influence the success or otherwise of strategic partnership need to be taken into account in the context of these forms of employer engagement.

In a recent article Lunnan and Haugland (2008) share a study that reinforces the broad criteria for success that Johnson, Scholes and Whittington define above. They find that although alliances can be very successful, many also fail, and look for the factors that may influence the performance of the alliance. They conclude that there are many factors that can influence both long- and short-term performance:

While short term performance can to a large degree be explained by access to complementary resources and the strategic importance of the alliance, long term performance is dependent on how the developmental process is handled. Developing lasting and successful alliances is a complex task that depends on the partners' ability to manage initial adaptations as well as their skills in handling the developmental process.

At the stage of strategic purpose they find that it is important that the level of strategic importance placed on the partnership is influential in its outcome. Thus the senior management support is crucial to the commitment that is necessary to support the alliance.

The research done with the sector groups showed that the strategic importance that was placed on these alliances by the differing organisations is different and the motivation for participation, although shared at a headline level, is perhaps not as well articulated in terms of clear outcomes and objectives. The employer interviews highlight not only the need for clearly articulated employer benefits, but also the issue of how the activity is going to be financed.

In the case of most of these sector groups, virtually all of the key players in their development were of middle-management status in their organisations. Although all their organisations were aware of and broadly supportive of the development, in most cases there was little in the way of a documented commitment in the form of either internal processes or the signing of a Memorandum of Understanding defining the 'terms of engagement'. There could be a danger that this lack of shared understanding as articulated in Gallacher's findings could sow the seeds of problems at some stage in the future.

As has been highlighted during the course of this chapter, the cultural differences between the commercial businesses and the public sector providers can be significant. Although it can be tempting to argue that the learning cannot be only one way and that the employers must also develop a better understanding of the HEIs, the bottom line is that, unless the providers are offering what the businesses want (rather than need), they will not bring their business to the public sector providers.

The third key element defined as being of importance is that of having a clear definition and achievement of performance levels. This needs to be done for internal purposes. How will the HEI know whether it is worthwhile allowing their employee to participate in such activity, if there are not objectives and outcomes agreed? What are the opportunity costs of the activity? It is also vitally important that all the partners in the activity share and agree these definitions, if the relationship is to be successful and productive.

The fourth key element for success is that of trust. As previously mentioned, some of the providers have worked together both on an individual basis and an organisational basis and this is a positive feature. The interviews certainly revealed a high degree of goodwill towards the concept of their partnership and a willingness to work together for both the benefit of the learners and the sector, as well as for the hoped for institutional benefits that would eventually accrue.

It is now important to return to the original rationale for this project – examining how best the public sector providers, be they universities or further education colleges, should view and manage their own participation in employer engagement activity.

It seems from the interviews undertaken with the providers that none of them have (or admit to having) much in the way of clearly articulated aims and objectives and outcomes for this activity. Participation in these sector groups could fit under any of the general headings of employer engagement, development of full cost commercial activity or fulfilling agendas around regional engagement. Nevertheless, however laudable or desirable participation in it might be, unless it is funded or can show an anticipated income stream against activity, at some stage hard decisions must be taken.

Partnerships and alliances such as those studied will usually come about in an incremental fashion through informal relationships, involvement in other partnerships or as a result of an initiative from some third party. Whilst there is clearly a period of incubation during which ideas are explored, waters tested and initial plans conceived, there must come a point at which the organisation must take an informed decision as to whether to commit to a particular project. Whilst not arguing that these things should be overly prescriptive or be too rigid and inflexible, there should be some sort of process or system that considers and evaluates the implications of the possible involvement in the partnership. No matter how creative and innovative an organisation or individual is, there comes a time when plans must be articulated.

Whilst all institutions will have procedures and criteria for the assessment and approval of academic delivery partners, there does not seem to be a parallel process for assessment and approval of potential partnerships or alliances. Whilst clearly some of the motivation for working in partnerships such as these may well be non-quantifiable and around fulfilling institutional or public sector agendas and objectives, not having a clear articulation of the rationale for involvement in these relationships can lead to potential problems.

- Uncertainty around strategic aim and its fit with wider organisational strategy. How can there be the high level strategic commitment necessary to make partnerships and alliances successful if there is not an articulation as to how it fits within the organisation?

- No objectives or ill-defined objectives for participation making assessment of its success difficult. There is a need for a clear articulation on issues such as whether this is ultimately going to be a commercial activity or if support for it is going to be funded from other sources

- Understanding of other partners' motivations – they are not all going to be the same as one's own organisation and having an understanding of their motivations will help to anticipate other partners' actions and reactions in particular circumstances as well as helping to develop mutual understanding and trust.

- No articulated envelope of resource (financial or otherwise) dedicated to the project making assessment of its value difficult.

- No risk assessment of implications of involvement, non-involvement or failure of the partnership.

None of the above is earth-shatteringly new. It is all fairly basic 'common sense' business principles. However, although HEIs are commercially aware organisations in terms of their own business models and core operations, this level of business sophistication is not particularly explicit in this sort of employer engagement activity. As with most organisations, the development of new product or service areas grows at different rates and the organisations' own management systems often have to play catch up to encompass the circumstances.

The models I have used during the course of this work could all play a part in developing such a framework, although how any individual HEI develops its evaluation process will reflect its own priorities and existing processes.

Although participation in third-stream activities is not new for HEIs, the importance of such activity, both in terms of participation in regional and national engagement and of the development of income streams, is growing. For organisations and departments involved in these case studies, participation in these sector groups does fit within their wider strategic aims. However, there does not appear to be a set of criteria or procedures through which an assessment of the impact of involvement can be made.

Compared to the highly controlled processes and procedures involved in course development or selection of academic partners, the involvement in this form of employer engagement is not well supported. During this research I have attempted to develop a framework that would help to develop an understanding of the motivations of potential partners which could help highlight some of the implications of involvement for particular partnership, and to inform a wider decision making process. Whilst not wishing to prescribe a method that would discourage involvement in this sort of activity, it would perhaps be of benefit to the HEI's to have a process that supported engagement, whilst ensuring appropriate 'due diligence' was undertaken. This would help ensure that the individuals involved in this sort of work were supported and empowered and also that the wider organisation made an assessment of the benefits and risks of each venture as well as ensuring that they could provide the appropriate support these initiatives required.

CHAPTER EIGHT

Business and Logistics Sector Activity

Sarah Gribbin

When YHELLN's strategic priorities were being set, much effort went in to ensuring that they reflected the needs of the sub-region, both in terms of building on and adding value to what had already been established and also focusing on economic priority sectors that were specific to the sub-region. Whilst 'business' is very broad and, theoretically, covers any and every commercial organisation in the region, 'logistics' is considerably more focused and easier to define.

The initial approach was very much a scatter gun one; contact as many people and organisations as possible and talk to them about what their priorities were and how they might relate to YHELLN's work. YHELLN partners, sector skills councils and businesses were contacted and it became apparent that there was a considerable amount of activity around the skills agenda within the logistics sector. Yorkshire Forward, the University of Hull and European Development Fund had recently invested a significant amount of money in the creation of the University of Hull's Logistics Institute, a regional centre of world-class expertise in logistics and supply chain management. In addition to this, several of the partner colleges were involved in either developing or delivering logistics programmes and the Sector Skills Councils for both logistics (Skills for Logistics or SFL) and for public transport (GoSkills) were very active within the region, as well as being professional bodies for the sector.

The early meetings of the business and logistics sector group prioritised their efforts and activities around working with Skills for Logistics, GoSkills and partners involved in the sector. Activities included developing links between partners and the sector skills councils, the development of foundation degrees and also the creation of a Regional Skills Academy for Yorkshire and the Humber. However, this emphasis on the logistics sector did not exclude other activities which included working with local schools and the council to develop the 14–19 Diploma in Business, Administration and Finance, and also the 14–19 Retail Diploma. Other areas of work included co-ordinating bids for the development of higher level skills provision within the City of Hull and bids for Enhancement Fund monies for logistics training. Another piece of work was carried out with a local employer to map skills training and progression within the organisation. The results of this work are due to be shared across the industry through GoSkills in the form of a case study and some awareness-raising materials for the business sector.

The single most substantial activity in this sector was very much the development of the Logistics Academy for the region and it is this initiative that will be described within this chapter as it highlights how many different stakeholders from the private and public sectors can come together to work with their own competitors and customers to create an organisation that will increase the size of the overall market and bring benefit to all.

Case Study: Logistics Academy Yorkshire and Humber

The aim of the Logistics Academy Yorkshire and Humber (LAYH) is 'to create a powerful, employer-led regional centre of excellence, to set new standards of how to design and deliver skills training for the Logistics Sector and to ensure more effective business outputs'. It will eventually provide employers and learners within the region access to the following services:

- A regional hub providing one stop shop services

- Career pathways; progression routes and core roles

- Sector-specific vocational qualifications

- Sector industry training framework

- Sector industry awareness programme

- Ambassador programme

- Placement programmes

- Mentoring

- Detailed labour market information

- Skills Passports

- HR advice service

- Training Quality Standard QS and Training Provider Charter

- Driver Certificate of Professional Competence

It will also act as an industry-wide spokesperson to help influence and inform regional and national policy, curriculum development and generally promote the sector.

It is a group of employers and skills training providers who came together in response to a tender from Skills for Logistics (SfL), the Sector Skills Council for the logistics industry. At this stage, although some Regional Academies were already in existence, not all of the details of the structures, guidelines and policies had been fully developed.

Shortly after the tender had been awarded a bid was made to Yorkshire and Humber East Lifelong Learning Network and West Yorkshire Lifelong Learning Network (YHELLN) for seed corn funding to employ a part time project co-ordinator whose role it would be to help identify additional sources of funding and help to set up the LAYH hub office. In June 2009 LAYH was formally launched by Digby, Lord Jones at an event hosted by YHELLN.

An important criterion of the tender (and in subsequent guidance issued from SfL) was that all the regional academies should be 'employer led' and, therefore, it was key that, although the driving force for the bid came primarily from the providers and the SSC, the employers needed to be fully engaged.

The winning consortium first came together in May 2006, although most knew each other and had worked together in various guises for many years. In fact, all through the development stage of the bid and the early days of the Academy no formal documentation or Memorandum of Understanding was in place between the partners and all partners devoted their time freely to the development of the bid.

In the early days the consortium recognised the importance of employer engagement at all levels and at all times during the life of LAYH. It was felt that previous initiatives within the sector had failed as a result of a lack of coordinated and consistent engagement from employers and that LAYH should not suffer the same fate. It was also seen to be important that employers of all sizes and from all parts of the region be involved in LAYH.

It was agreed that employers would be represented by the LAYH Employer Group and that they would be in the majority on the LAYH Board and on the national Executive Committee. An employer would Chair both the Board of Directors and the Executive Committee. The responsibility for ensuring effective and on-going employer engagement was intended to rest with the LAYH Manager, a position, which at the time of writing, is yet to be filled as funds have not yet been secured for the post.

At the time that the original consortium was forming (2007/8) there was relatively little in the way of formal written guidance on structures and processes from SfL centrally other than the original tender document and the main source of guidance came from the SfL Regional Manager. As a result of this, different Regional Academies in different parts of the country have developed in slightly different ways and their methods of operation are slightly different. However, as increasing quantities of guidance and draft policies are being produced by SfL nationally, it is anticipated that these regional differences will diminish rather than increase.

Whilst it was always the intention that the regional academies should be self-supporting, the lack of formal National Academy status has meant the SfL has not had the resources it had originally hoped would be in place to support its regional academies. This factor has placed the embryonic Regional Academies in a somewhat precarious financial position, as they had no initial direct financial support from the parent organisation. This situation has now been exacerbated by the announcement in 2009 that the 3rd round of bids for National Academy Status has been postponed and, hence, there is no immediate possibility of direct funding from SfL. However, in an attempt to compensate for the lack of National Academy status, SfL have launched a series of central initiatives to help support the work of the Regional Academies, including a centralised course finder database and a centralised telephone service for all enquiries. The intention of these initiatives is to reduce the initial cost burden in the regions.

Since its formation the LAYH has successfully bid for funding from YHELLN and the West Yorkshire Lifelong Learning Network (WYLLN) and has secured sufficient seed corn funding to employ a part time project co-ordinator and buy in some temporary part-time support from Hull University's Logistics Institute to enable it to start functioning. Hull University has also provided it with office accommodation and support equipment. Hull College, the lead institution in the original consortium bid, has also continued to support its COVE Manager's day-to-day involvement in LAYH.

In summary, the possible sources of funding are:

- Delivery Spoke Providers annual membership fee. This would need to show value for money. The Providers would need to see the benefits of membership in terms of business that they could not have otherwise got in their own right. On what basis should fees be set – size of institution, volume of business coming from LAYH?

- Employer contributions. Employers may already subscribe to other trade bodies and would need to see the benefits to be gained from membership. Particularly in the current economic downturn, will businesses invest scarce resources in this?

- Joining Fee – issues as above

- Pay as you go – who would bear the cost, the employer or the provider? Would the additional cost result in the training being more expensive than if sourced directly from the provider?

- National, regional, sector sources of funding – as public purse strings tighten, this potential funding source is also likely to reduce.

The challenge of ensuring the economic viability of LAYH is considerable with the existing funding stream terminating in less than a year. It will also need to consider its own viability and alternative forms of organisational structure and modes of delivery should fresh sources of funding not be available.

With a committee structure and the part-time co-ordinator now in place, communication between all the various stakeholders is relatively smooth and routine. There is good attendance at meetings from a wide range of stakeholders, including employers, providers, Yorkshire Forward and other interested parties. Not only have formal channels of communication been set up, it is clear that informal channels are also being established. Although some partners had previous working relationships, others had not, and there is early evidence of new working relationships being established. Partners are regularly informed of events and opportunities that arise within the sector.

YHELLN has also helped to provide electronic support to help manage the communication task at the regional level and early discussions have taken place at a national level concerning possible use of e-systems that have been developed to support learners and their possible role within SfL.

Tangible evidence of the support that LAYH has amongst its partners was the response, at very short notice, to submit a partnership bid for some regional funds for training in the logistics sector. Although the bid was unsuccessful, the concept of joining together to submit a partnership bid under the umbrella of LAYH was enthusiastically embraced by a large number of the providers.

In the first round of applications by providers to become recognised hubs for delivery, most of the providers involved successfully submitted bids. The number of important regional employers who have joined the Board is also pleasing and demonstrates how the employers are keen to engage with issues around skills even in a recession. A marketing plan has been developed and a series of events are being attended that offer LAYH the opportunity to promote its services and providers.

Perhaps the biggest challenge to LAYH is that of sourcing an ongoing funding stream as soon as possible. The reduced support from Skills for Logistics centrally and the current economic climate do not bode well.

However, the lack of funding could provide the opportunity to re-examine the service delivery model with a view to redesigning it to take advantage of the technological opportunities that currently exist to support access to information and support for organisations and learners.

If funding is to be provided by charging members for services, the product offer will have to be one that is valued by the members and its benefits very clearly articulated. The early enthusiastic response and the commitment made by regional employers to LAYH seem to confirm that it has a bright future.

Another clear opportunity open to LAYH is to continue making strategic links to other organisations involved in the logistics sector. This would help to open up opportunities for joint bidding and strategic alliances, as well as providing a forum for the logistics sector to have a collective voice within the region. It could also play its role in other sector wide initiatives that would impact on logistics and the supply chain industry.

The consensus of those involved in the case study was, generally, that things had gone well and, with the exception of the funding issue, problems had been relatively minor. The team involved in the development of LAYH had been able to respond to the situations as they arose. Particular successes included the partnership working between the providers who could have viewed themselves as competitors but worked in a very positive and supportive manner with each other. Equally positive has been the response of the regional employers who have become involved to help steer and lead through membership of the Board.

It is always easy with hindsight to identify what one might have done differently. It is still early days for LAYH, however, it is fair to say that without the involvement of YHELLN its development would perhaps not have been quite so easy in terms of the provision of resources and funding. In the current economic climate, it is not unreasonable to conclude that YHELLN has bought LAYH some time to get itself established and promote its activities.

The experience of supporting the development of this sector-based group also helped to complement the development of other sector-based groups in the areas of engineering, digital media and health and social care. By coincidence rather than design, all four of the sectors identified by YHELLN as being of importance have created groups. Although the impetus for these groups all came about in different ways and the emphasis of their work manifests itself in different ways, they all share similar aspirations and aims. They all want to act as a forum to share experience, develop ideas, inform policy, support their members and highlight the need for and worth of higher level skills by offering opportunities to potential learners and employers. The creation of these four groups during the lifetime of YHELLN has not only allowed the Higher Skills Team Leaders involved in each of them to share experiences, but has also allowed for some research to be done with the groups and the experience of each of them to be produced. This has been a valuable and insightful experience for YHELLN and for others within the lifelong learning sector.

However, the concentrated involvement in LAYH has possibly meant that other opportunities may have been missed. One such area of work that has not had a lot of attention has been the area of generic 'business' leadership and management. In the early days of YHELLN time was spent with partners mapping and reviewing provision in this area. What was evident from that work was that the generic area of higher level business provision was fairly well covered by traditional programmes, such as degrees, HNC/Ds, foundation degrees, short courses and in-house training. There was not much demand for work in this area when delivered as generic 'business studies'. It is clear from research into organisations about skills provision and future shortages that there is demand for leadership and management training. The demand does seem to be in this area of leadership and management skills rather than the more functional 'business studies'. The demand also tends to originate from identifiable sectors and concentrated effort on these may have been more effective, for whilst many of those involved in the delivery of leadership and management curriculum may view what is delivered as being non-sector specific, those in organisations often want something tailored to their own circumstances. With hindsight, it might have been effective for YHELLN to have created a cross-cutting work stream for leadership and management which would have tapped into this sectoral demand. This approach could have provided a resource for all the key sectors within the sub region in a format that was sufficiently flexible to be adapted to suit the needs of each.

All four sector groups have also gained an insight into how the institutions involved manage the wide ranging processes and aspects of employer engagement, including the 'softer' aspects. This unexpected insight revealed that the processes and systems involved in managing this work do not appear to be formalised or standard even within the same institutions. This has afforded the opportunity to explore possible working with other universities, looking at issues relating to employer engagement and third-stream activity.

CHAPTER NINE

Creative Arts

Sarah Humphreys

At its inception YHELLN established four priority areas on which to focus its activities, selected because of their strategic importance to the sub-region. One of these was Creative Arts, a broad and diverse area encompassing activities ranging from those with a traditional 'crafts' focus through to those with a strong technology focus, such as Digital Media.

Higher Level Skills team leaders were allocated to each area with a very open brief to further YHELLN's aims and objectives in relation to improving opportunities in vocational Higher Education. The YHELLN project had a limited lifecycle of three years in which to be effective, and it seemed that a targeting of effort towards attainable goals in the timescale would be pragmatic. For Creative Arts the approach in the first instance would be a consultation with partners to pull together shared interests and goals.

Meetings were convened with representatives from partner colleges and other stakeholders, and it became clear that key issues for the priority area concerned curriculum development, employer engagement and progression. Partners had an interest in developing and redeveloping the curriculum in line with the foundation degree framework and in engaging employers in identifying and supporting curriculum opportunities. There was a desire to improve progression both internally and externally, and some very creative thinking around how this might best be achieved was exemplified by one of the first creative collaborative project proposals to be presented and agreed. This was WAX, the Wearable Art Expose.

This project was a collaboration between Hull College, Grimsby Institute and North Lindsey College, an ambitious two-phase undertaking comprising a Wearable Art competition, culminating in a day-long event, and a subsequent travelling exhibition of the work. The idea was to raise visibility and aspiration and to encourage progression through the public nature of the project. Schools, colleges and other stakeholders entered the competition, often working on the brief within their own curriculum time. Garments were selected under a number of themes and those chosen were modelled at the event itself to an audience drawn again from schools, colleges and other stakeholders. The pride and burgeoning confidence of those students involved was inspirational. Trade stands and portfolio clinics brought the business world into the mix, offering a glimpse of the vocational outcome for those completing studies. Media coverage together with a selection of garments formed a travelling exhibition which brought the quality and excitement of the event to partner colleges. The project successfully brought together aspects of progression and employer engagement in an exciting and inventive way. Partners were convinced of the merits of an event of this type and funding has now been secured to ensure the sustainability of the event.

The development of appropriate progression pathways and opportunities was a challenge and priority for all YHELLN partners. The context was that progression rates in many parts of the area have often been lower than regional or national averages, the economic downturn is damaging students' confidence in their futures and YHELLN covers an extensive geographical area, which is largely rural. Alongside the WAX project were other initiatives which drew together a range of approaches to address these problems, such as taster sessions (one day) and bite-size modules (10- or 15-credit Level Four modules), referred to collectively as staged engagement. Yorkshire Coast College, for example, had an excellent response to their offer of taster sessions in Digital Media which were mainly skills focused but gave an insight into subsequent bite size modules, such as Digital Imaging. Although many saw the sessions as a leisure activity, some were seeking a new career path. A key aim for the college was to show people what was possible and raise their enthusiasm, even though many started with low self-esteem and low aspirations. Students who had never considered Higher Education were drawn gently and supportively into HE programmes.

Internal progression from FE to HE was an issue for all partners, and work took place on establishing liaison activities and HE taster events to form a meaningful part of agreements at every level. At Hull College a school-wide Higher Education taster programme was conceived comprising a series of regular calendared events. Opportunities were made available for all Creative Arts Level Three students to choose from a range of stimulating 'hands on' sessions in a choice of subject areas and to spend a day working alongside Higher Education students and staff in their studios. The peer group experience offered by working with students currently studying at Level Four was seen as an important part of the progression experience. The day was well attended with positive feedback, although on reflection it was felt that the Further Education students would have benefited from more in-depth information about the programmes they were opting to sample. Although it had been common practice to organise external Higher Education promotional events, for example, attendance at UCAS fairs, this had been neglected internally because of the assumption that Further Education students would attend Higher Education Open Days. It became obvious that this was not sufficient and that students would like an information session at their own base. Accordingly, an internal Higher Education Fair was scheduled at the Further Education students' own premises.

Week long bite size modules were also offered to 'internal' Level Three students as a pilot scheme. The module incorporated an introduction to broad based study skills in order to support the transition from Further to Higher Education together with some practical studio based experience as a taster of a particular subject area. Feedback suggested that this experience had instilled the confidence in participating students to consider progression to undergraduate study, where they hadn't previously considered this as an option, and some are now enrolled on programmes of their choice.

Curriculum development was another key area for consideration within the Creative Arts area. A number of projects were undertaken in order to refresh, review and expand the curriculum offer, some of which have now reached fruition through the enrolments of students onto new Foundation Degrees and BA (Hons) in September 09. Hull School of Art and Design undertook the development of an innovative suite of programmes, including Digital Media Journalism and Art and Design for the Public Realm, which were specifically directed at an industry 'niche' and were the result of extensive employer engagement in the development process.

Digital Media Journalism started life as a Foundation Degree Broadcast Journalism, but after feedback from a range of employers, including Hull Daily Mail and the Press Association, it became clear that there was a need for journalists who could film, photograph, source and write up an article and place it online in an appropriate form, people who would be multi-skilled practitioners for the media and public relations industries. Drawing on the strengths of the Schools' New Media provision curriculum was written to meet that need, resulting in a Foundation Degree which is amongst the first of its type in the country. Art and Design for the Public Realm was developed in place of a more conventional 3D Design programme following extensive consultation and in response to the extensive regeneration programme currently taking place in Hull. The curriculum concentrates on environmental issues in an evolving city and enables students to help shape the creative and practical use and aesthetics of public buildings and spaces. These new Foundation Degrees go beyond the customary range of art and design programmes to target recent developments in industry and to resonate with regeneration initiatives across the region.

When the University of Lincoln moved its provision from Hull, the Hull School of Architecture was lost to the city. An architecture 'hub' initiative conceived at Hull College was to bring back this key curriculum area. Employer meetings drew together architects from a wide range of practices, many of whom had qualified in Hull. They were unanimous in their support for this initiative and offered tangible help, for example, through providing work experience opportunities. The 'hub' initiative was unusual in that it drew together Engineering and Construction and a Foundation Degree: Architectural Technology with Creative Arts and a BA (Hons) Architectural Design programme were introduced. Employer consultancy played an essential part in developing a curriculum which would have to subscribe to the professional standards and rigours of ARB and RIBA. Several part-time programmes were developed specifically to meet the needs of those already in employment in the workplace or those unable to follow a full-time two- or three-year course. Flexible delivery models were explored, for example, combining evening study with summer schools. Foundation Degrees in Graphic Design and 3D Design and Crafts were written to replace existing HNCs and HNDs, with an extended curriculum encompassing work related learning. Specialist

3D Design and Crafts pathways in Jewellery and Ceramics drew on staff expertise and a strong resource base to offer students new degree options which could be completed in two years following an extended academic year model. A new Foundation Degree in Digital Media was written in response to industry interest in part time study in Games, Web or Interactive Media. The intention for the future is to include Adobe professional accreditation for production skills as an integral part of the programme, as directly relevant to the requirements of the sector.

There has been a greater recognition of the value of embedding professional qualifications in the Creative Arts curriculum, particularly as part of bite-size modules. During 2008 Yorkshire Forward funding enabled staff from schools and colleges across the sub-region to participate in a series of Adobe Certification training sessions, delivered by the IT Foundry in Sheffield. These staff in turn cascaded their expertise by training student groups who successfully gained certification in a suite of Adobe products. This opportunity to gain a professional qualification was welcomed by staff and students alike and, in particular, was seen as an excellent portfolio and curriculum vitae feature for those about to leave education for employment. Discussion has taken place regarding the embedding of this certified product training within bite-size modules at Level 3 as part of the Creative & Media and IT 14–19 Diplomas.

In order to develop and support relevant curriculum and to offer client-related experience to students as appropriate to vocational education, employers must be consulted and engaged with throughout the curriculum development and delivery process. Increasingly, employers are bombarded with requests to attend engagement events and, as a result, many are badly attended. YHELLN supported a project which took a different approach in building a relationship between education and industry. HumberMud (media, usability and design) is a networking group which was initiated by an employer in conjunction with YHELLN and Hull School of Art and Design with the objective of creating a network of practitioners, educators and business users within the region and an environment for collaboration and innovation. The group provides a forum and lobbying body for those practitioners, businesses and educators with the local authorities and local planners and acts as an interface in general to the creative industries in the region. It raises the profile of HumberMud members across the region with practitioners, businesses and educators with similar interests from outside of the region. Finally and importantly, it also provides a 'step up' for recent graduates and current regional students by providing links to business and potential future employment.

HumberMud hold a monthly networking and knowledge event featuring industry specialists and local talent, which is disseminated globally through the HumberMud website and podcasts. The events have proved a great success, with attendance from representatives of the many and diverse local businesses working within the creative and digital industries sectors exceeding expectation. They have also provided a focus for staff and students of the YHELLN partner colleges. A rich variety of both student and commercial projects have been showcased and there has been healthy debate regarding the Digital Media industry. Speaker topics have included, for example, documentary filmmaking, funding and collaborative bidding processes, BBC big screen projects, together with iPhone and Apps developments. Initially, the network events took place only in Hull, but the group has extended recently to include South Bank events which are coordinated by East Coast Media at Grimsby Institute. YHELLN also sponsored Hull Digital Live, a one-day conference which attracted excellent high-profile speakers to the city and was attended by a cross-section of business with both academic and student representation.

A broad-based creative industries group has developed over the last year with a steering group drawn from education, business and Hull City Council. This Creative and Digital Hull initiative has been welcomed by businesses, with good representation at events organised to date. Funding has been made available in the short term to develop and publish a business directory and to establish an online presence through which members can communicate and be kept informed of developments. This group is lobbying for the establishment of a Media Centre for Hull, and a feasibility study is in progress.

Creative Arts partners have developed a range of excellent resources in support of these curriculum, progression and employer engagement agendas, including a project to develop and podcast video based learning materials and the development of 'Critit', a regional online showcase and employer resource. The intention of Critit is to enable students and graduates to showcase themselves and their work through a visual online portfolio, to allow companies to post company details and portfolios and to bring these two sections together through a free job listings feature. Companies can post jobs details, be they full-time remunerated positions, casual freelance opportunities, or work experience. They can also search for talent to fill their vacancies, people who actually want to work within the region. Those looking for work within the region can examine company profiles and identify those they would like to work for. There is also an events listings feature which, for example, could be used to promote Degree Shows. There any many job sites and portfolio sites, but what differentiates Critit is that it is regional and specific to the broad-based Creative Arts.

It is imperative that students seeking work in the Creative Arts sector have a strong and well considered portfolio. To this end Critit includes a regular 'Industry Experts' feature comprising interviews with industry representatives and including portfolio tips and advice on getting into the industry. Social networking features are deployed to enable flexibility and sustainability of this section. The process of carrying out interviews is also a strategy for growing the company content of the site, which is one of the challenges for a resource of this type.

As with the WAX project, another consideration for Critit was the raising of aspirations for those considering a Creative Arts education at any level and for those currently studying who may progress to a higher level. The creative portfolios on the site showcase talent, but also demonstrate the professional standard of work produced as an outcome of the education process. An aspiration for the resource is further to develop social networking features to enable discussion between those showcasing their work and those interested in Higher Level study, informal 'buddying' for example. Another aspiration is that of graduate retention – there is a vibrant Creative Industries sector in the region but with poor 'visibility' in some areas. By creating what is effectively a very public and visual companies directory, Critit can address this issue and highlight to students the excellent opportunities available locally and regionally.

The Creative Arts area gave rise to all these and more projects and developments. Whilst these were exciting and had a positive outcome, there was inevitably a series of barriers to be faced along the way. Partnership working, identified as a key requirement in the proposal process for all YHELLN projects, was also one of the key challenges.

The WAX projects relied on collaboration between many stakeholders; schools and colleges (staff and students), community groups and individuals who produced and gathered competition entries; businesses and education who ran the professional aspects of the day-long event; and students, school children, college staff and the public who organised the fashion show itself. Most importantly, staff from Grimsby Institute, North Lindsey and Hull Colleges collaborated in the overall organisation and management of the whole project. The geographic area itself was a challenge, proving a logistical nightmare for arranging meetings, collating and selecting entries, moving costumes and models from location to location, organising rehearsals and so on. One institute had to take the lead in each phase of the project, with Grimsby Institute leading on the competition and day-long event and North Lindsey leading on the subsequent travelling exhibition. Each of the YHELLN partners has aspirations, with targets to meet, networks to build, and employers to engage – inevitably, competition exists and can prove a barrier to fruitful partnership working and some aspect of this division crept in to the smooth running of this project. However, this was perhaps more keenly felt by those deeply involved and, seen from the outside, the project was an exemplar of collaborative working at its best.

Implementation of successful progression strategies and agreements brings a different set of problems to solve. One dimension of progression, from the student perspective, is to do with aspiration-raising, signposting, and clarification of options. From the college partners' perspective it is also about raising visibility of provision, curriculum development to provide progression pathways and, again, about building partnerships. There are many other complex issues bound up including the competition between partners, but our purpose here is to follow a number of case study examples.

Hull College had a strong and extensive Creative Arts provision at both Further Education and Higher Education levels, and these were housed in separate buildings. Feedback from those Higher Education students who had progressed internally suggested that the process of moving to another building and working alongside other undergraduate students had given them a sense of 'HE-ness' which they valued. Equally, the different locations could prove a barrier to progression. Rather than offering promotional events at the Further Education site, it was assumed that students would attend Tasters and Open Days in the Higher Education building. However, after running various progression activities it became evident that the Level Three students would welcome and feel more comfortable with an initial introduction to degree programmes in their own location prior to the 'Higher Education experience' events. The barrier to dealing with this effectively in the first place was one of the perceptions for which the YHELLN project enabled actual evidence to be gathered, analysed and actioned.

The College generally offered a well-established and harmonised curriculum providing 'feeder' routes from Further Education through to Higher Education. However, for the undergraduate in New Media provision these pathways were not in place, as these programmes had been transferred over from the University of Lincoln. In order to support recruitment for the New Media area it was necessary to develop a Level Three Interactive Media provision which was expected to feed through to the degree programmes. Equally, the reverse applied in the development of degree programmes which reflected a growing demand from pre-degree students, such as the Foundation Degree in 3D Design and Crafts, or from those in employment, such as the Foundation Degree Digital Media. The problem of curriculum (and therefore progression) 'gaps' was thus being effectively managed through the YHELLN supported curriculum development process.

Many new programmes were produced in the Creative Arts area during YHELLN's three years. Effective curriculum development relies firstly on considerable research in establishing both potential need for and the viability of new programmes. The write-up and subsequent validation of the programme of study then relies entirely on staff time and expertise. Many college staff have considerable teaching commitments which leave little space for the process of programme writing. Equally, whilst all are subject experts, some may have little experience of programme development and the associated (and sometimes daunting) quality procedures. Engagement of employers in the development process is hugely beneficial but also time intensive. Whilst some YHELLN partners have strategies in place for allocating time and support to all of these processes, others do not, and this gap can prove a barrier to HE in FE developments across all subject areas. YHELLN project funding has enabled new curriculum development, for example, through offering replacement teaching hours, so staff can concentrate on programme writing and involving employers in that process. Support offered by experienced YHELLN staff has also played a part in growing the extensive portfolio of new curriculum products which have come to fruition during the three years of the YHELLN project.

Another challenge for YHELLN partners, again across all subject areas, is the marketing of their provision. There is some reliance on the traditional prospectus and website as a main means of promoting programmes and some partners do not have the means to extend this model through offering, for example, differentiated marketing material for new or different markets or by employing approaches such as social networking or other online strategies. Building relationships with feeder schools and sixth form colleges is an important factor in local recruitment and this responsibility often sits with academic staff, as does the promotion and organisation of events such as taster days, whereas in large universities a different team would usually take responsibility for this role. YHELLN funding and staff expertise have been utilised to address this issue via various partner projects.

Employer engagement is the life blood of vocational Higher Education. This applies not only during the curriculum development process, but also in actual programme delivery where work-based or work-related modules often form a 'core'. The model for Creative Arts tends to be that of students working on 'live' briefs as an integral part of the curriculum rather than undertaking formal work placements, although these are sometimes possible and appropriate. One challenge that derives from this is the management of expectations between all parties involved. It is imperative that any projects enable the students to fulfil the learning outcomes for the module the client work sits within, so much care has to be taken in ensuring a suitable level of complexity and challenge in each project. The client must be made aware that, whilst they have a key input into the process (other than assessment), the outcome may not be entirely to their specification. For example, there may be problems about time scales; the shape of the academic year structured by semesters with specified hand-in dates and so on may not fit comfortably with a live project timescale. Intellectual property rights and, in some cases, confidentiality must be considered. Industry mentors may need suitable training. Students have to respond to the challenge of working within very tight parameters and, in some cases, taking a given role within a team. The list could go on and on and academic staff responsible have a complex task in balancing and managing all these various needs and expectations. An important part of developing a new curriculum is to consider all these issues and put strategies in place together with training as appropriate.

Management of expectations is a theme which also related to the employer networking projects outlined earlier. Was their prime function to do with business-to-business or education-to-business partnerships? For those in industry the priorities are to meet other company representatives and to forge business relationships. For educators the focus is on understanding the business sector and forging suitable curriculum in response. For students the chance to network with businesses and to make links for future employment is important. A possible conflict of interest came to light during the early days of HumberMud and could have caused a barrier in the running of the group. However, much common ground, for example, an interest in graduate retention in the area, was also established. The formalisation of the group through a constitution, committee and steering group helped in arriving at a shared vision.

In conclusion, The Creative Arts area undertook a range of ambitious projects, weaving together key areas of curriculum and resource development, employer engagement and progression. Collaboration between multiple stakeholders was achieved throughout, difficulties which arose have been circumvented and lasting working relationships have been founded through this process. Many of the projects are really at a starting point rather than a conclusion at this stage and strategies are in place to sustain them beyond the YHELLN project. Ongoing review and reflection will refine these initiatives for the future.

CHAPTER TEN

Higher Education in Engineering and Construction

John Deverell

The content for this chapter has been influenced by quotations attributed to Lord Baker, Secretary of State for Education from 1986 to 1989 that were published in the *Guardian* newspaper on 31 August 2009. (Curtis 2009)

> 'English education over the age of 14 has always failed to deliver technical education'. (Baker 2009)

In my opinion, English education has always delivered excellent technical education and training and continues to do so. Nowhere is this more apparent than in the YHELLN region. Across all the YHELLN partners there is a real commitment to developing and delivering excellent education and training.

> 'If we are going to build new power stations and Crossrail and new [airport] terminals we don't have the technicians at all levels. It's not just bricklayers but at every level of the building trade. (Baker 2009)

Engineering and Construction industries require technicians, but there have always been ample education opportunities for technicians at all levels. Progression is well understood: bridges and ladders have always been in place. Where labour shortages do exist, they are more often a consequence of market forces, financial constraints and economic factors. There is no point in developing technical education if the jobs in industry are not there. Research by the Humber Economic Partnership shows a national decline in these industries. Where jobs do not exist because of the decline in engineering and construction industries, it is difficult to convince young people that there is a future for technology in this country.

> 'We want our lads and lasses to start with basic stuff; electrical circuits and welding. I think this is the way forward for technical education in this country'. (Baker 2009)

The 'basic stuff' is not electrical circuits and welding, but numeracy and literacy. Technical education is demanding and is underpinned by these prerequisites at all levels. Unless they are in place, it is impossible to improve access to Higher Education in engineering subjects. Fortunately, most of the educational and professional bodies are well aware of this. It is easy to be complacent, but in most aspects HE provision in the region in Engineering and Construction is in good health. There are strong indications that it will get even better.

Full-time provision is, in the main, provided by the University of Hull. The Department of Engineering in the University of Hull continues to maintain its high reputation as a provider of full-time MEng, MSc, BEng and BSc awards in Mechanical, Electrical and Electronic Engineering. There are gaps, most noticeably in construction and civil engineering, but to a large extent this is not a new phenomenon. The transfer of the Hull School of Architecture to Lincoln by the University of Lincoln meant that the region lost a vital resource, including a number of construction-related courses. However, over the last two years Hull College has developed the 'Architecture Hub'. Its immediate aims will be to service the needs of the architecture profession, but in time it will be able to expand into the areas of construction and the cross-over subjects, such as Construction Operations Management and Quantity Surveying. Here it will meet the already very successful FE provision in construction that is presently provided by Hull College.

Part-time provision has expanded considerably over the past few years. Much of the increase has resulted from close collaboration between employers in the regions and the Higher Education Institutions. An exemplar of good practice is the link between the University of Hull,

Humberside Engineering Training Association (HETA), and Corus at Scunthorpe. This provides seamless progression from apprentice training through part-time Foundation degree awards delivered in part on-site, to the BEng and MEng awards at the university. In the other HEIs there is a similar story of enterprise and innovation. In December 2007 there were three Foundation degrees in engineering and construction running in the region. Two years on, there will be well over twenty validated awards available for part-time study. In addition, there will be two new full honours degree awards and one new, work-based learning MSc. Much of the Foundation degree provision replaces existing HNC/D awards. However, it demonstrates a widespread programme of course and curriculum development that has occurred in each of the YHELLN partner colleges. Given the nature of the Foundation degree awards, this has also involved a far greater involvement with employers and sector skills councils than has ever been attempted before. For instance, completely new provision for the region in Chemical Engineering is provided at the University of Hull by a new part-time Foundation degree designed to meet the needs of employees in the local chemical and petro-chemical industries. This development is part of a wider project run by the Department of Chemistry, called the 'Working Higher' project. (See www. heacademy.ac.uk) This is an innovative new HEFCE funded project that joins employer federations, such as Humber Chemical Focus and Sector Skills Councils, such as Cogent (www.cogent-ssc.com) and Semta (www. semta.org.uk) to the university. Its prime objective is to develop a new suite of Foundation degree awards in collaboration with employers in the region.

The most gratifying aspect of all this activity is that all colleges from the large to the small have shown a willingness to get involved. There has been a very high level of collaboration and co-operation from which all have benefited. For instance, in the development of the foundation degree in Building Services Engineering, eight HEIs across Yorkshire and Lincolnshire were involved, each helping the other, observing and learning from the shared good practice. This award is now available to be shared by all who participated in its development.

A considerable amount of time has been invested by YHELLN partners in the development of Foundation degrees, as a route into higher education for vocational learners. Although a Foundation degree may be a stand-alone qualification, it is more likely to articulate with a named degree programme and, therefore, must contain those prerequisite elements that define the degree award. It should include work-based learning at all stages of the award. The characteristics of the award are particularly beneficial for part-time learners.

The rationale for Foundation degree awards in full-time mode is unconvincing. Foundation degrees can provide a stepping off point for those who wish to defer their studies. However, this facility already exists in most Honours degrees, when, on leaving the course, students are normally awarded a Diploma. The sequence: certificate, diploma, degree is current world-wide. It is possible that future students will find the mixture of awards confusing and their progression routes and pathways unclear. For a more positive view of full-time Foundation degrees, see Foundation Degree Forward's website (www.fdf.ac.uk).

The stand-alone aspect of Foundation degrees has value when it covers situations that frequently occur in vocational contexts. Training stops when the particular skills-defined needs of a trade have been met. If education does continue progression pathways often lead to another discipline, usually some aspect of management. If there is a skills gap, it is here that the gap is widest. There is much evidence from engineering and construction employers in the region that awards that bridge the gap between trades and professions are needed. A related factor that has yet to be satisfactorily resolved is the mismatch between the awards and apprenticeships. Most employers willingly support their apprentices though two years of part-time study. Some refuse to support a third year, for the very good reason that their apprentices have reached the skills level appropriate for their jobs. Consequently, there is a very high 'drop-out' rate at the end of the second year of some part-time Foundation degrees in the region. This has an effect on retention rates and may become an even greater problem if ...'College and university courses...' become... ' subject to new league tables based on how many students drop out...' (Curtis 2009). Polly Curtis was reporting on preliminary comments made by the chief executive of the UK Commission for Employment and Skills, (UKces). The rationale behind UKces' reported statements appears to be so contrary to normal methods of maintaining standards that much of the good work behind Foundation degree development may be wasted.

The most important, attractive and defining characteristic of the Foundation degree award is the work-based learning content.

> 'Authentic and innovative work based learning is an integral part of Foundation degrees and their design. It enables learners to take on appropriate role(s) within the workplace, giving them the opportunity to learn and apply the skills and knowledge they have acquired as an integrated element in the programme. It involves the development of higher level learning within both the institution and the workplace. It should be a two way process... Work-based learning requires the identification and achievement of defined and related outcomes'.
> (QAA 2004)

The way it is described by QAA is splendidly idealistic but is difficult to achieve in practice. The main problem is integration, since it places such demands on employers that even large organisations, where training and mentoring is part of the company's structure, would find it difficult to implement. For employers in small companies it is impossible. Similarly, most academic institutions are not able to operate one-on-one staff to student ratios in more than a few modules. There are some very good attempts at meeting QAA's objectives. In the region, many of the Foundation degrees in engineering or construction are validated by Leeds Metropolitan University. Of the sixteen, fifteen-credit modules that comprise their awards, four are defined as Work Based Learning modules and four as Personal and Professional Development modules. The remaining eight modules may have work-based elements but are not specifically tied to WBL learning outcomes. Both engineering and construction curricula fit this framework very easily. Project and Design modules have much more relevance and interest when the project topics are derived from the workplace. Similarly, the content of the PPD modules such as IT, and Personal Skills can easily be tailored to each student's role at work.

Most of the engineering and construction Foundation degrees validated so far are very ambitious and a great improvement on the HNC awards that they replace. It is hoped that the delivery of the awards is as good as the design, in particular, in the ways in which work-based learning operates. Learning Contracts between learner, tutor and mentor can only properly be done on a one-to-one basis. However, excellent quality procedures that monitor the education process are in place. These appear to be flexible enough to help staff in the implementation of the work-based learning aspects of the awards.

There has been considerable effort and energy expended in an attempt to make vocational education and training providers more responsive to the needs of employers. For instance, the Foundation Degree Forward website contains much excellent, common sense advice. In my experience and from two years' observation and involvement with the local colleges that deliver engineering and construction awards, many of the employer engagement strategies they describe are already in place, because networks and relationships are inherent to the delivery of this type of part-time education and training. The first and obvious link is the students themselves. They can see both sides of the education process better than either employer or tutor. Also, all colleges operate some form of industrial liaison process and many spend time in industry assessing and teaching students on the job. While there is nothing much wrong, there is no reason why it should not be continually monitored and improved where necessary. The implementation of the Foundation degree awards provides an excellent stimulus for reviewing approaches to employer engagement. The most important factor, by far, is the introduction of work-based learning. As noted already, it is not easy to deliver work-based learning in the ideal way. However, any work-based learning model must inherently involve tutor, student and mentor in a collaborative process. Once this is functioning properly, the groundwork for employer engagement has been achieved.

Over the last few years there has been a far-reaching review of awards in all of the YHELLN partner colleges. More course and curriculum development has been undertaken in the last two years than in the previous ten. This has led to staff having to face a number of challenges. In colleges where HE awards are only a small fraction of the overall provision, that is, all of the colleges in this region except the University of Hull, FE staff are starting to work at an educational level of which few have extensive experience. Foundation degrees should be degree-worthy and the context, environment and resources that support the award should be fit for that purpose. Staff teaching on an award that leads to a professional qualification should themselves be qualified to at least that standard. Most staff still work on FE contracts with remission from teaching duties for course development. Most are paid on FE rates and have teaching loads that are based on FE norms. This means that staff in FE Colleges have to develop and deliver HE awards without the flexibility afforded to staff who work in universities.

Considering the challenges, the progress that has been made is amazing. One of the major factors that should be praised to the rooftops is the large amount of collaboration and co-operation that has occurred over the last two years. It is to be hoped that the larger colleges and the university will continue to help the smaller colleges to develop and manage HE awards.

The Progression Engineering Centre is a YHELLN supported initiative aimed at meeting some of the higher skills needs in engineering, construction and manufacturing industry in the region. It was developed as a response to several stimuli that reached YHELLN in the summer of 2008. Firstly, the employer groups in the region were getting increasingly worried about a perceived skill gap in the areas of engineering and construction. This gap was a problem that would possibly hinder the anticipated investment in the region, in particular, the new biomass power stations planned for the south bank of the Humber. A similar gap was identified by one of the sector skills councils, the ECITB, for the development of their engineers. Whilst many large employers are able to provide the support to engineers to develop the appropriate skills, small- and medium-sized employers often do not have the resource or the capacity to be able to do so. This has led to large numbers of potential engineers being disadvantaged in terms of their own professional development. The knock-on effect is a workforce that is under-qualified. The second stimulus came from discussions with the ECITB and their support for the 'Gateways Project'. (See www.engc. org.uk) This then led to the Engineering Department at the University of Hull engaging in discussions with the Engineering Council, resulting in the decision to develop an MSc in Professional Engineering along the guidelines suggested by the Engineering Council. The project has initially been limited to the needs of employees and employers to fulfil the requirements for Chartered Engineer (CEng) status with the Engineering Council. On successful completion of this first objective, the project will be expanded to meet the needs of Incorporated Engineers. The general objective of the Professional Engineering Centre is to:

'Provide a service for aspiring professionals in engineering that will link all aspects of formation and threshold competencies: academic qualifications, work-based learning and responsible professional experience.'

The centre will eventually work with all levels of engineers from graduates to time-served apprentices to help them through the process of becoming accredited as Incorporated or Chartered Engineers with their relevant engineering institution. It will provide a work-based learning MSc qualification leading to chartered status including mentoring for all learners and electronic storage for the required portfolios of continuing professional development (CPD) and academic study. In addition, training for mentors will be provided. There will also be a full range of stand-alone modules of training and CPD available. Links with partner colleges will increase progression opportunities and engagement with employers will create a framework for the development of their staff. The following paragraphs outline the basic elements of the Centre in more detail.

The MSc in Professional Engineering is a work-based, part-time award that, subject to the accreditation processes of the appropriate professional engineering institutions, will meet the standard demanded by UK-SPEC (UK Standard for Professional Engineering Competence) for registration as a Chartered Engineer (CEng). The award provides work-based progression opportunities for those working in the sector who have not attained the academic requirements for CEng registration. The award will be available from Sept 2010 and will comprise modules chosen from the full-time MEng degree programmes at the University of Hull together with a substantial amount of work-based project work. The student will be in employment in the engineering profession have a BEng(Hons) or equivalent qualification have an employer who is prepared to support the student's studies and provide the resources and opportunities for day study and work-based project work and have ready access to the internet both at home and at work. Throughout their studies each student will be supported by a mentor. This mentoring service may be extended for as long as is required, but will normally have the objective of supporting the learner through to registration as a Chartered Engineer (CEng).

Mentors will be Professional Engineers and will be from both the University and industry. The mentoring service will extend beyond the completion of the academic requirements for registration as a professional engineer and will cover all areas defined as responsible professional practice (www.pd-how2.org). The mentoring of employees towards CEng or IEng status is an innovative development that has never been attempted before. The service will help each person to design and develop an individually tailored programme of study or experience. The programme will be designed with the active co-operation of the person's employer. It will recognise and, where appropriate, accredit previous learning and experience, maintaining the person's record to meet the learning and competencies specified by the appropriate professional engineering institution. In addition, the mentoring and repository service will be available to any applicant holding any suitable engineering award who requires a Professional Development Audit (PDA). A repository service will store and manage each employee's record of achievement of engineering competences.

The Centre will also provide a range of short courses that can contribute to the student's Continuing Professional Development. Courses are already available through the Engineering Innovation Institute, EII, the industry-facing part of the Department of Engineering. The EII also provides opportunities for industrial skills based training that are particularly aimed at employees of small companies. The Centre will also approve those accredited CPD activities that were obtained elsewhere. All users will have access to the repository service.

Part of the remit of the Professional Engineering Centre is to encourage, foster and link with other degree developments in the region. The Department of Engineering already supports and validates Foundation Degree awards at Doncaster College, North Lindsey College and East Riding College. The centre will continue to work with other HEIs in the region to accredit and validate awards, such as Foundation Degrees, and to establish progression agreements in the field of engineering. All students on these awards will have access to the mentoring system and will be registered by the repository service.

The repository service will be an interactive VLE (Virtual Learning Environment) based system that deals with the administration of student achievement, examination boards, awards boards etc for students at partner colleges, students doing accredited CPD and all persons included in the mentoring process. This ambitious project was initiated by YHELLN and external funding has been secured. The JISC Project, 'Personalised systems supporting IPD and CPD within a professional framework: CPD-Eng' started in April 2009 and will run for the next two years. The systems developed will be able not only to store large quantities of data, but also to be secure yet flexible enough to offer access to those who need it. Considerable progress has already been made. User needs and user interactions have been defined. These are interactions between students, mentors, employers, tutors, other HEIs, professional bodies and other educational institutions. Figure 11.1 shows the way in which the learner interacts with the other participants. All stakeholder needs are defined in relation to user interactions that are required by any individual embarking on a professional career in engineering. The repository system thereby aims to meet all the types of user interaction that take place as a formative engineer progresses to registration as a chartered engineer. This project has huge potential for other professions who also need a secure but interactive storage system for ongoing CPD activities. It is not surprising that the CPD-Eng project has gained widespread national and international interest.

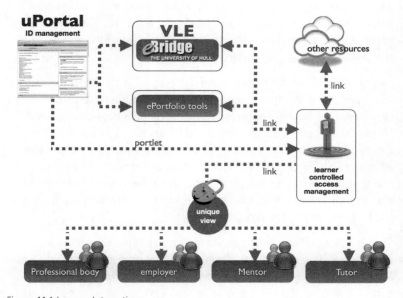

Figure 11.1 Learner Interactions

The development of the Professional Engineering Centre is well under way. It is initially focused upon the needs of those persons who wish to reach CEng status. It is proposed that in the near future, the Professional Engineering Centre will provide and advise on similar flexible pathways towards Incorporated Engineer (IEng) status. In due course, the facility may be extended to cover EngTech qualifications. Both of these ventures would be in collaboration with other engineering education providers in the region. The Centre will then provide a service that covers all aspects of engineering education. It has been very gratifying to see the way in which the Department of Engineering, YHELLN and the Hull University's Knowledge Exchange have worked together to coordinate the growth and development of the Centre. They have successfully pooled their expertise and resources to help support the Centre with each party ensuring that employers and partners they have involved in the Centre are kept informed. Not only are the benefits accruing from the JISC project immediately transferable into other areas, but also the concept of the Professional Centre could easily be applied in any other disciplines where professional registration was necessary or desirable.

The first project, 'Developing an employer-led Foundation degree in Construction Project Management' was mainly funded by AimHigher and Foundation Degree Forward. YHELLN provided a small amount of funding to support colleges in the curriculum development aspects of the project. The project was innovative in that the project leader, Jackie McAndrew, worked with employers in the region and with the Construction Skills and SummitSkills Sector Skills Councils to develop the award. The Higher Education Institutions were not actively involved until the later stages of the project. The project followed a process of establishing links through over 200 regional companies. These were gradually reduced to those companies that would actively help to determine the desired content for the award. A core group of nine construction companies with eight client organisations finally produced an indicative module list with the content defined for each topic. A similar analysis was undertaken to determine the student profile. The most typical student was described as a mature, non-traditional learner, probably with much experience and qualified to Level 3 through a vocational award. It was also established by the group that modes of attendance should be flexible, although part-time day and evening was the most favoured. It took less than four weeks to produce a definitive document to meet the requirements of the validating body, Leeds Metropolitan University (LMU). The course material fitted very easily into the LMU scheme, including their prescribed requirements for four work-based learning and four personal professional development modules. The project is summarised and published on the Foundation Degree Forward website.

There were additional benefits as a result of the project. The strong focus on both work-based learning and personal and professional development was deemed to be directly relevant to their business needs. The former was consistently seen as an important factor and most employers were committed to getting involved in mentoring. Contact with a large number of companies identified potential students. The project also produced marketing material that was used by Hull College. also In addition, it identified a list of associated needs for the region, particularly a general need for support to help non-traditional learners. In particular, it revealed that there was a lack of provision in Building Services Engineering, Contract Administration and Management, Design, Civil Engineering, Construction Contracting and Planning in the region. All participants were pleased with the result and agreed that the process had been extremely valuable.

As a direct result of this project, YHELLN commissioned a similar follow-up project. The immediate aim was to design a Foundation degree award in Building Services Engineering. The second aim was to encourage the colleges to use the employer engagement model that had been used in the previous project. Two lead providers were identified, Doncaster College and Grimsby College of Further and Higher Education, with Hull College acting in a supporting role. In the event, the employer engagement model was not used to the same extent. The main reason was that SummitSkills had produced an excellent Foundation Degree Framework Specification that had already covered employers' requirements. (SummitSkills 2008) The framework was mapped to UK SPEC and supported mechanical, electrical or commercial job functions, or combinations of these. Each college devised variations on the SummitSkills framework that were then shown to employers for their approval. The paths of the two colleges then diverged, with two distinctly different awards being developed. At Grimsby Institute of Further and Higher Education, with Leeds Metropolitan University being the validating partner, the team decided to offer limited options in Refrigeration, Air Conditioning or Heating and Ventilating and to provide a mathematics pathway for those students who had aspirations to further degree awards in engineering. The award at Doncaster College was validated by the University of Hull. In their Foundation degree awards the work-based content is spread more widely. The Doncaster team decided to provide two routes – one electrical and one mechanical. The proposed models were discussed amongst employer groups and also, at Doncaster, with prospective students. Most of the students studying at present on the first and second years of their HNC awards welcomed the opportunity to move to the Foundation degree award. The process was significantly different to that used for the Construction Project Management award. There was much more divergence than had been anticipated, but, as this was as a result of variations in employer demand, it is to be applauded. All three colleges will recruit students to the new awards in September 2010.

YHELLN staff are part of the national team that is working with Construction Skills to devise another Foundation Degree Framework Specification. This is in Construction Operations Management. Their particular responsibility is for Employer Engagement and Marketing of the award.

The 3D/4D project is based on the 3D technology owned by Kognitiv and the Digital Knowledge Exchange based at Doncaster College. The system and software that they have developed uses 3D images that are fully interactive, so time-varying systems can be modelled, using visual representations that are close to the real thing. The project that the Higher Skills Team members have been involved with is based on the Building Services Science module that was developed for the Foundation degree in Building Services Engineering. This module was chosen because, from the learners' point of view, it is probably the most boring of the modules in the award. Also, its content is easily transferable into other 'science' modules in other awards. The objective is to design and devise exciting and stimulating material that would relate directly to the delivery of the module. After considerable debate it was decided to use 'the room' in 'the house' as a place in which all the learning outcomes for the module would be based.

The package thus provides an exciting visual peg on which the teacher can hang the more boring bits, such as mathematical modelling, analysis and assessment, as he or she wishes. The student gets a fully interactive package that can summarise and enhance the whole of the module. The package will be provided on a CD or on the web. This will lack the 3D effects but is still fully interactive. The 3D equipment required for delivery of the full experience will be available for use by all the YHELLN contributing partners. College tutors are already being trained in its use. This is another excellent example of innovative practice being developed and shared, thanks to the stimulus provided by YHELLN. What would Lord Baker make of this?

'English education over the age of 14 has always failed to deliver technical education' (Baker, 2009).

Perhaps Lord Baker could be invited here, so that he may see for himself that technical education in the region is delivering a first class service.

CHAPTER ELEVEN

YHELLN Research

Nick Hooper

Out of 30 Lifelong Learning Networks (LLNs) set up, only two LLNs created a full-time research post. YHELLN established a post of Work Strand Manager for Research, Continuing Professional Development and Evaluation, and Staffordshire, Stoke-on-Trent, Shropshire, Telford and Wrekin a post of Research and Data Manager. However, this does not reflect the true role of research in LLNs, as all LLNs carried out activities which could be viewed as research. Rather it is a reflection of how each LLN chose to structure and staff itself.

YHELLN adopted a wide definition of research as embracing any activities providing data, information, or analysis in support of YHELLN aims and objectives. A similar definition was later adopted by the national LLN research network when it began collecting and collating information on research activity by LLNs.

The YHELLN Business Plan provided for the appointment of a Work Strand Manager for Research, Continuing Professional Development (CPD) and Evaluation and set out the following objectives for the work strand:

- Develop existing research opportunities (to include training in education-based research methodologies) for practitioners (teaching and support staff, especially in the FE sector and staff in work-based learning, etc) with respect to vocationally-based HE learning opportunities in the sub-region.

- Determine the current range of relevant research-based activities locally, regionally and nationally, including that conducted by LSDA and the HEA.

- Work with key external organisations, e.g. relevant SSCs, RDAs, employer and trades union organisations, other LLNs and key research-based organisations, to ensure that modes of delivery of HE-based vocational learning opportunities are relevant to learners in meeting the higher skills needs of the sub-region and that information in respect of new approaches to learning reaches the widest possible number of potential learners and their employers.

- Research the current range of relevant teaching and learning strategies, especially work-based, to ascertain examples of good practice.

The first task of the Work Strand Manager was to turn the remit given by the Business Plan into a plan of action. To do this, a number of principles were established:

1. The role of the Work Strand Manager would be to support research, wherever it occurred within YHELLN, not to control or restrict it.

2. The research programme would be determined by the YHELLN partners.

3. The impact on the research capability and capacity would be as important as the immediate use of any research outputs.

4. Where possible, YHELLN-funded research projects would be undertaken by staff of partner FE colleges.

The aim from the start of work under this Work Strand was to leave a legacy in the form of a volume of research output, a network of researchers and an enhanced capacity and capability to undertake research across the partnership. The YHELLN deliverables, against which this aim would be measured, were the number of research studies completed and disseminated.

Based on the above principles, a research action plan was developed, taking into account:

- The perceived research needs of YHELLN, as identified by Work Strand Managers, Curriculum Focus Teams (later renamed Higher Skills Teams), partners and associate partners.

- Opportunities for the development of research capacity and capability across YHELLN partners, at both the institutional and individual level.

- The involvement of YHELLN partners in the development of research plans and project proposals through comment and participation.

- Where possible, activity and functions which may be considered research would take place across the YHELLN structure and staff. Only if resources were needed that were not available within the YHELLN network would projects be contracted out.

- Research activity could be initiated by any member of YHELLN. Projects would be developed using the YHELLN Project Management Framework and included in the research register maintained by the Work Strand Manager.

- Internal and external projects would be managed under the YHELLN Project Management Framework. The process included peer review and a project management group. Projects valued under £1,500 would be managed under a simplified procedure.

- Outcomes of research would be shared/published as widely as possible, including a YHELLN series of publications.

- Findings and outputs would be disseminated through CPD as well as other appropriate activities.

The process of developing research projects was iterative and progressive, initially driven by the Work Strand Manager but, progressively, allowing for the involvement and ownership by staff of the YHELLN partners. The process started with the drawing up by the Work Strand Manager of a list of potential research topics. Some of these were drawn from the YHELLN Business Plan, which identified modes of delivery and teaching and learning strategies as potential topics for research. The initial reviews of needs continued with a series of discussions with YHELLN partners and staff. This produced a longer list of potential subjects for research:

1. Employer engagement

    a. Market research for new provision developed by Curriculum Focus Teams, later renamed Higher Skills Teams

    b. Dissemination of 'outside' research through CPD

    c. Projects:

        i. Research into employed learners

        ii. Market intelligence/foresight

        iii. Learning experience of employed learners

        iv. Research into HEI/employer relationship

        v. Employer attitude/barriers to HE

        vi. Employer attitude to accreditation

        vii. Returns to training

    d. Case study of best practice

    e. Development of capacity

2. Widening participation and student diversity

    a. Employees' attitudes to vocational learning

    b. Employees' attitudes to HE

    c. Vocational learners' attitudes to HE

    d. The demand for HE from vocational learners

    e. HE admission or rejection of learners with vocational qualifications, including reasons for rejection

    f. Teaching and learning strategies

        i. Current range

        ii. Development – including retention, achievement, inclusiveness

3. Educational partnerships

    a. Documenting and mapping partnerships

    b. Mapping progression agreements

    c. Mapping modes of delivery

A series of literature reviews and research surveys was considered, to provide background academic, factual and pedagogical information to inform YHELLN and to support research projects. In the event, many topics had been covered by published literature reviews. In addition, adopting the alternative approach of including brief literature reviews as a part of each project ensured that the projects were embedded in the literature and helped to develop good practice and a research culture and capability. The purpose of this list was to suggest possible topics and stimulate consideration and discussion, leading to proposals for projects. It was not intended to limit projects to topics on the list, or that all the topics should be the subject of projects.

Two meetings, open to all staff of YHELLN partners, were held to discuss the research action plan and to identify research topics to be funded by YHELLN. These meetings also helped to identify those YHELLN partner institutions which were keen to support research and develop their research capability and capacity, as well as identifying staff likely to undertake projects. Following these meetings, the Work Strand Manager for Research met with those who had expressed an interest and advised on research project proposals. A small committee was set up to assess proposals and award funding. This helped to ensure that the award of research projects followed the general YHELLN project proposal process and the project criteria. It also provided an audit trail for any future audit.

Provision was made for proposals for:

- Small scale projects, such as literature and research surveys. These were seen as likely to be from individuals, including those beginning a research career.

- Pilot projects, with a view to developing larger projects and funding bids.

- Larger collaborative projects led by experienced researchers.

In the first round, participants were encouraged to submit small proposals, typically for £1,500, to allow a member of college staff to devote half a day a week for one term to a project. This had a number of benefits:

- It did not impose a major burden on college staffing.

- It provided a block of time which staff could devote to a project.

- It identified staff who had the interest and ability to carry out larger projects.

- It identified the colleges which would in practice make time available for research.

- It provided a number of researchers with experience and for many provided the basis on which they could seek funding to continue their research.

In the second round of funding, opportunities for projects were again identified in collaboration with partners. However, the award process was changed. Three clear themes of research had emerged. Proposals for larger projects within these themes were requested. Each project was expected to be collaborative, based in and led by one YHELLN partner institution. The experience of the first round of small projects provided a guide to the partners and individuals likely to be successful in managing, undertaking and completing larger projects.

The themes were:

Theme 1 – Relevance to learners of different aspects of progression.

Theme 2 – Employer and learner engagement with HE providers and vocational learning.

Theme 3 – Understanding new pathways.

YHELLN supported over 130 projects in total. The range of subjects reflects the YHELLN Work Strand activities and the Higher Skills priority curriculum areas. Many of the projects fall within the wide definition of research as embracing any activities providing data, information or analysis in support of YHELLN aims and objectives. Not all of them were grounded in the academic literature, and research and the development of research capacity and capability was not a recognised aim of all YHELLN projects. All YHELLN projects were supported by the Work Strand Manager Research, when requested, and research projects were supported by other YHELLN staff.

The research programme led to a total of 35 research projects being accepted for funding. Of these 35, 28 have been successfully completed. The remaining seven were agreed but have not reported, either because the time required to undertake the project was not made available to the staff involved, or the staff left their post.

The YHELLN Research Work Strand aimed to support the work of YHELLN by facilitating research. At the same time, implementation of the research strategy sought to develop the capability and capacity for research in the YHELLN partners and across the network.

The research programme which evolved from this and the research outputs demonstrate the achievements which are possible within a limited budget, both in terms of output and developing capacity and capability. Support has been given to researchers at varying stages in their research careers. Research outputs with direct application to supporting vocational learners have been achieved.

The YHELLN research experience has highlighted issues as well as opportunities associated with the approach taken. As expected, short, low-budget projects proved to be more appropriate to the FE model of high contact (teaching) hours than to the HE model of teaching, research and scholarly development. The dominant issue for research in FE remains time. However strong the commitment to research, inevitably teaching will take precedence over research in the allocation of staff time. Allocation of time for research tends to be easier to agree and more likely to be realised where HE in FE forms a larger share of activity, and more so where institutions are seeking HE awarding powers. In part, the allocation of time to YHELLN research reflects the early stages of transition from the delivery of HE by an FE institution to the achievement of awarding status by that FE institution.

The YHELLN programme also helped institutions to identify staff with an interest in pursuing research, and by providing an opportunity for a small-scale project those staff were able to confirm their interest in research and managers were better able to assess the research capability and capacity of their staff. In addition to research experience, opportunities were created for staff to gain experience in various forms of dissemination, including publication and conferences.

The programme has shown the benefits of collaboration in research. It has also highlighted the significant cost involved in collaboration between researchers in the early stages of their research career, having to take on issues relating to collaboration alongside managing their own research, negotiating time while at the same time undertaking the research.

On balance, the YHELLN research programme achieved its objectives. All partners had an opportunity to undertake projects, and all had at least one project approved. In the event, not all projects were completed, either because staff left or as a result of pressure on staff time. Projects delivered valuable information to support vocational HE and at the same time strengthened the research capacity and capability for the future.

CHAPTER TWELVE

Delivering User Value: eSystems

David Sowden and Jason Reed

Let's suppose the worst case scenario happens. You put up a website and no one visits or you try and market a course and few want it. You do every marketing thing imaginable and there just isn't much of an audience. You spent months putting this together and your monetary rewards are few. So what do you have at the end of the day?

Unless the eSystem delivers user value, then you have only a redundant technical concept – without the user there is no solution.

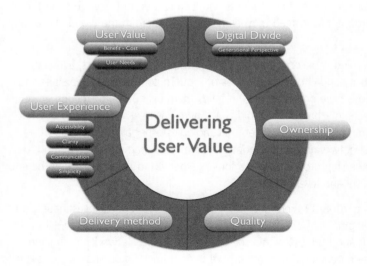

Figure 12.1 Delivering User Value

This chapter's mission is to highlight the importance for e-infrastructures and technologies (referred to in this document as eSystems) to create value for the lifelong learner. From experience, solutions are often started from a technology-first perspective, which is fundamentally the wrong way around when the goal of an eSystem is to create value for the user.

The chapter is, therefore, driven from the user perspective covering: the user value, user experience (and the importance of accessibility and the associated delivery methods). The chapter will also examine four cross-cutting themes: The Digital Divide, Marketing, Ownership and Quality.

Finally, the chapter provides a tool to use in planning the development of an eSystem that summarises the key points of the chapter.

The world we live in is constantly changing. The main changes in the last decades have included: computers gaining omnipresence; a society diverse in culture, education, and socio-economic levels; a high-skilled workforce needed in the majority of work places; a highly competitive business market; the appearance of new educational technologies; and decreasing students' interest in such traditionally prestigious subjects as physics, maths and engineering.

Learning is changing as well, especially the technologies of learning. e-Learning means that students and lecturers do not have to sit in the classroom, but instead they learn from anywhere in the world and at any time.

e-Learning is becoming very popular with Lifelong Learners, allowing flexibility and choice. Thousands of modern companies, universities and colleges have online courses. It helps them distribute knowledge among learners in a broad and rapid way. There has been also growth in what is commonly known as Web2 technologies especially in the area of social networking sites. Adoption curves vary dramatically by region, but membership growth in all regions is expected to have peaked by the end of 2009 and level out by 2012.

During 2008/09 there have been two extensive reports investigating the development of eSystems (Reed J and Sowden D; Haywood M, Nixon I, Bell R and Burke J.) within the Lifelong Learning Networks in England. These have shown that there have been numerous duplications of systems and products and scope creep.

The user value (benefit-cost) is the value that an eSystem creates for the lifelong learner and how this relates to their needs. The needs of the lifelong learner are both those that are directly related to their learning journey and also their requirement for an environment that engenders confidence and enables the lifelong learners to focus on their own personal development goals. This requires functionality, stability, security, clarity and affordability.

To achieve this, it is important that the eSystem design process is started from the user-first perspective. This will ensure solutions deliver true user value.

Therefore, fundamental knowledge of the user is important, along with possible learning styles. Those involved in the development of eSystems need to ask the question, who are the learners and users?

Through research within many of the established Lifelong Learning Networks within England, a user who sees learning as a lifelong journey will have some of these traits:

- Have positive self esteem

- Be accepting of others

- Be perceptive and understanding

- Be capable of interacting effectively

- Have problem finding and solving abilities

- Be creative and independent

- Discovers and develops personal passions

- Wants to impact the world in a positive way

- Have good communication skills

- Undertakes personal reflection.

There is more than one type of learning that our lifelong learners will use. A committee of colleges, led by Benjamin Bloom (1956), identified three domains of educational activities:

Cognitive: mental skills (*Knowledge*)

Affective: growth in feelings or emotional areas (*Attitude*)

Psychomotor: manual or physical skills (*Skills*)

Trainers often refer to these three domains as KSA (Knowledge, Skills, and Attitude). This taxonomy of learning behaviours can be thought of as 'the goals of the training process.' That is, after the training session, the learner should have acquired new skills, knowledge and/or attitudes.

Asynchronous learning resources (ALRs) developed as interactive courseware for the World Wide Web are receiving increasing attention because of the ease with which they can be accessed by lifelong learners at the time, place and pace of their choosing. Knowledge-based ALRs are critical for developing the knowledge base essential for problem solving. Problem-based ALRs are especially attractive because of their emphasis on the higher-order cognitive skills of analysis, synthesis and evaluation. Computer-based interactive courseware can be developed to enable lifelong learners to acquire the entire range of cognitive skills contained in Bloom's taxonomy.

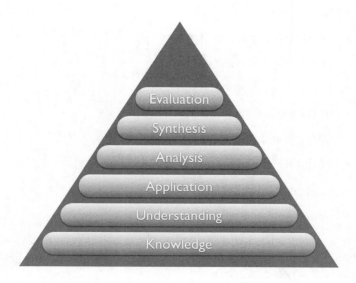

Figure 12.2 Bloom's Taxonomy

Graphic-intensive instructional modules sandwiched between an introductory statement and a formative quiz are used to constitute lessons designed to develop knowledge and comprehension. Practicums composed of problem statements and a series of questions for leading learners through a disciplined process of inquiry are designed to enable learners to acquire higher-order cognitive skills, including application, analysis, synthesis and evaluation.

The way a lifelong learner represents their identity changes according to circumstances. Different contexts require a different identity, each of which is expressed in a different way and provides different information. All of these contexts have ways for an individual to establish their identity and, just like the physical world, they will have a variety of *digital identities*, expressed in different ways. Today, however, there's no consistent way to 'model' the physical world and reflect this portfolio of digital identities.

Different kinds of digital identities will always be necessary—no single identity will suffice – and neither will any single identity provider. The solution is not to mandate a single system for digital identity, but find a coherent way to use multiple digital identity systems. Using these Web services' technologies, it is possible to define a consistent way to work with any digital identity created by any source and using any identity technology.

CPD-Eng is a JISC-funded project providing an innovative, personalised infrastructure that will support the work-based learner through a new suite of flexible pathways to professional qualifications for the engineering professional, integrating real and online worlds and enabling learning to take place 'whenever and wherever'. Significantly, without creating the right amount of value for the user, a system will not be well adopted no matter how good the communication strategy is. Before developing a system there needs to be a real clarity of purpose for the development and the development needs to be tested against this as it progresses.

A definition of value is benefit – cost. Understanding this is really key to developing a successful software solution for the lifelong learner.

The benefits of the system come through functions provided by the software that enable the user to perform new tasks or old tasks better.

This has often been defined as either a Decision Support System (providing information to support a decision) or an Online Transaction Processing System (a way of performing a basic transaction using a software system). This means identifying some functions that provide benefit to the user that is significant compared to other alternatives. The benefits can be due to:

- The individual functions

- The combination of functions available via this one tool (integrated functionality)

- The fact that so many functions are available in one place

- The stakeholders connected to the functionality

  - Peers

  - Customers (in the broadest sense)

  - Suppliers (in the broadest sense)

- Security, speed and stability compared to alternative solutions.

The costs of a system, in addition to finance, really need to be examined. From experience, applications more often fail as a result of not considering the Total Cost of Ownership (TCO) of the system.

The costs are generated from:

- Financial cost to the user (The Internet is now full of free software)

- User experience

  - Ease of use (based on their prior learning and experience, how much can a user just work out for themselves)

  - The 'look and feel' of the system (does it have an appropriate aesthetic to it?)

- Does it provide the user with confidence in both the technical fulfilment and the way that it communicates to the user?

  - Security (Is it secure; does it communicate security to the user?)

  - Stability (Is it stable and reliable; does the user feel this?).

In addition to the general position of any system there are particular benefits and costs that relate to the lifelong learner. These benefits include:

- Enabling them to find learning

- Supporting their individual learning (content through to self-reflection)

- Enabling them to find and develop accreditation and qualification.

The lifelong learner will need to do the first two above points during their life. Ironically, the third aspect is the one that often spawns the development of systems, as they are nearly always developed by academic institutions. In reality, accreditation and qualification is not always a requirement for lifelong learners, unless they have specific professional requirements that drive them. User experience is about the user interface: accessibility, ergonomics and clarity (visual, oral, written communication).

Accessibility is massively important, as it is the only aspect of user experience that involves legal compliance. In addition to compliance, there are extensive guidelines that suggest ways to support users' needs. There is a balance that needs to be considered in implementing an eSystem so that it serves the needs of the whole user community and this involves making a compromise between different stakeholder requirements.

For a successful user experience it is vital that, when designing a user interface (UI), the structure satisfies the levels of functionality and clarity required by the user. Information architecture addresses questions such as:

- What are users' primary goals and how can they achieve them using the application?

- How do users get from place to place?

- What rules exist that users have to work around?

- What is the optimal scope of the application's feature set?

- What is the application's search mechanism?

Since September 2002 the 'The Special Educational Needs and Disability Act' (SENDA) has extended the 'Disability and Discrimination Act' (DDA) to include the education sector. As far as web-based applications are concerned, you should not disadvantage any disabled visitor to your application by offering information or services that they cannot access. There is nothing in the SENDA or DDA legislation to say exactly what makes an accessible website, but the general consensus is that the (World Wide Web Consortium) 'W3C Guidelines' will be used as an industry standard.

The justification that web-based applications are accessible because they 'follow standards' contains a serious fallacy; specifically, the assumption that standards support accessibility.

Using the recognised current HTML or XHTML standards set by the World Wide Web Consortium (W3C), is a fine practice and certainly should be maintained. Using correct syntax and following a standardised method of communicating information is always a solid best practice. However, this should absolutely not be taken to mean that following these standards is the same as applying the principles of web accessibility.

Web standards only provide accessibility to the degree that they have been designed to do so and the guiding principle behind standards development has not generally been to support accessibility. Web standards have been designed purely to establish a set, correct method of using the underlying code, whether presentational (CSS), structural (XHTML) or behavioural (ECMAscript.) In many (most) cases, web standards do not in any way require best practices, they merely require conformance. Does this necessarily mean that the standard is wrong or right? No, not as such. Different standards support different needs: it is important to keep distinct the purpose of the standard.

Around 1910, the German architecture and design school 'Bauhaus' employed this simple creed: 'Form follows function, ornament is a crime'. Bauhaus didn't exactly teach web design and they didn't deal with print ads, email campaigns, or flash-based interfaces, but the basic principle will work for any area of design. Simple and functional design will essentially make things easier for the individuals who use, or are subjected to, the design. When design is based on the required function, form comes along naturally. For example, have you ever used or visited a website where there is so much art and motion that you can't tell what is going on, or what you should even be clicking or navigating on? One can encounter sites like this quite frequently. Sometimes the sites are actually quite aesthetically pleasing, but they've missed the point of why they even wanted to make it 'pretty' in the first place. By following the rule 'Form follows function, ornament is a crime', we can start to break down what is necessary and what is not.

First off, one has to determine what the function is. If one does not know what the function is in terms of the user, then it will be difficult, if not impossible, to make it easier and simply to use. It is vital to analyse the functions required by our lifelong learner, produce the case, prioritise, then focus on making those functions easily usable and accessible. Determining what is superfluous to your design is simpler than you think. Ask yourself this question about every element of your design: Does this compliment or complicate my function?

There is often a desire to fill in every 'white space' or 'hole' in your user interface. This does not mean you cannot use all the space you are provided with, but give it some breathing room, areas where the eye can rest and linger. By allowing your layout to be evenly and moderately spread out, content and navigation will be much easier to view and use for your users.

Examine all your content and ask the question: Is it really needed? Where should it be placed that would make the most sense? Is it helping you or hurting you? Too much verbiage or call to action can clutter and confuse users. Make your content and actions clear and concise.

Is the design layout logical? Really think about how a user is going to navigate through the user interface. Even though you may think what you're doing is logical, YOU aren't your users. Test.Test. Test.

Quality is achieved by evaluating the whole eSystem against all of the areas and requirements to be considered as part of evaluation and continuous improvement in delivery. Quality doesn't cost money. Poor-quality products and services pile up extra costs for a provider. The 'cost of quality' isn't the price of creating a quality product or service. It is the cost of NOT creating a quality eSystem. This could heavily impact on the user confidence in the solution developed, losing adoption and integration, and would lead to costs to regain confidence. In short, any cost that would not have been expended, if quality were perfect, contributes to the cost of quality.

Don't assume you know what the learner wants. There are many examples of errors in this area, such as 'new Coke' and car models that didn't sell. Many organisations expend considerable time, money and effort determining the 'voice' of the customer, using tools such as customer surveys, focus groups and polling. Satisfying the learner includes providing what is needed when it is needed. In many situations, it is up to the learner to provide the provider with some of the requirements.

A solution will be aimed at a particular market. It is important to consider an approach that will be well suited to the target demographic and possibly utilise the ability to provide different approaches, devices and interfaces to meet the different demographics. There needs to be some consideration of those who have access to technology and those who don't. In addition, the skill levels, geographic locations and generational perspectives need to be considered. Economic growth is increasingly driven by the skill of the local workforce and, more specifically, confidence and competence in using digital technologies.

So it should be frightening that nearly 50 per cent of the European population does not use the web and a significant percentage of homes do not have internet access according to recent reports. Sadly, the development of applications and eSystems only serves to enhance a two-tier system in which, as we develop services, we design them for the IT literate, while maintaining secondary systems for those currently excluded.

As the middle class and articulate are relative early adopters of new services and emerging knowledge, they tend to make full use early of web-based systems. Likewise, if we do not begin to develop applications of digital technology designed to address inequality, we shall reinforce the digital divide by default.

A key challenge is that access to technology will become necessary within Maslow's hierarchy of needs as individuals progress. Increasingly, digital technology will become key to them, starting with wealth, or at least work.

Figure 12.3 Maslow's Hierarchy of Needs

But there is still a considerable overlap between social exclusion and digital exclusion. So we need to be creative in developing targeted digital applications in health, if they are to help bring people into the digital age rather than act as a further barrier to use. Our providers need to commit investment in the use of digital technologies to tackle inequality, including partnerships with those more skilled in adapting digital to new markets than we are. We will have to invest in technology beyond the interventions of the recently announced national 'Action Plan for the Digital Economy'.

The new barrier is basic ICT skills, now being addressed through voice technology, increasingly intuitive technology and assertive investment in schools, with 90 per cent of 16–24-year-olds now ICT familiar, if not fully literate.

The key barrier now is attitude and interest. Our most disadvantaged communities are often our most disappointed, with learned low expectations and limited appetite for new experiences. We really need to understand what the added value of new technology might need to be, for people to wish to use it. While digital technology has a huge amount to offer everyone, paradoxically it could have disproportionate benefit for the currently disadvantaged. The Digital Britain White Paper (HMSO 2009) sets out the importance of the Digital Economy to the nation's economic future, and how it will drive future industrial capability and competitiveness. It comprehensively makes the case that the UK's communications infrastructure and increased Digital Participation are key to building a 21st-century knowledge economy and must be considered essential objectives, if we are to become world leaders and reap the benefits of this rapidly transforming sector.

Technology needs to be subservient to the needs of the lifelong learners and appropriate to a number of different factors. There is not one way of providing a solution that is perfect and the 'best' solution is not just about the selection process, but about responding and developing once the solution is deployed. The solution selected needs to consider the technologies, people and other resources available to meet the user's requirements.

Many researchers have documented the increases in potential learners worldwide, drawing attention to the social imbalance in access to higher levels of education. There was/is a perceived need to develop much more comprehensive, flexible, innovative and radical solutions and strategies to engage with these new learners. These strategies will/have necessitated a 'radical change' in conventional educational thinking, methods, organisations, structures and practices. In other words, a new approach has been needed, touching on all aspects of the educational process:

- Changes in learning needs (more people wanting to learn different things)

- Problems of financing (reduced funding, demands of more effective use of resources (staff etc.)

- Increased concern about democratisation and fairness (social equality, elimination of socioeconomic, gender and geographic inequities)

- A perceived need for closer ties to day to day life (lifestyles), harmony between education and culture, relating education to work, lifestyle, ecosystem, common values

- A need to change teaching and learning strategies

  - There has been a realisation that educational providers need to review their teaching and learning strategies to enable the flexibility required for the lifelong learner. Providers are encouraged to allow individual customisation of learning, allowing reactive solutions to training and personal development needs. At present, funding and reporting requirements often contrive to discourage and hinder this type of flexibility, especially when eSystems are utilised.

- New emerging forms of communication (other than the written printed word)

  - New methods of educational delivery

- Changing demands of work – retraining

- New career patterns

- Home-based work

- Changing clientele for education – increasing numbers, especially in mature-age students, resulting in both work and career changes.

By starting with user value we have a good basis for the future adoption of the solution. It is really important to make sure that the value hypothesis originally generated has been tested out on lifelong learners at the beginning and is reviewed as the solution develops. If the solution provides value, then it is important to find a way to market/communicate the existence to potential new users.

Adoption is often the result of:

- The user seeing the potential of something 'new'

- Popularity with peers

- Additional functionality

- A portal to other places allowing a seamless experience to the user

- Personal skills and requirements.

In addition to the individual lifelong learner adopting the eSystem it is essential for sustainability that someone takes ownership of the delivery (It could even be owned by lifelong learners in a wiki environment). Intellectual property might be considered also. Recently there have been debates concerning the capacity of a lifelong learner to source learning from a range of providers, allowing the learner to be in control of their own learning, accessing possibly the best resources and content from around the world.

Social networking sites could, in their next generation, facilitate this, allowing individuals to create a personalised learning environment accessing learning from numerous locations.

Figure 12.4 Checklist for Delivering User Value

Define Scope		
Action	**Questions**	**Factors**

1. Develop an understanding of the user	What are the problems/ needs of the lifelong learner (user)?
	
	What is the current provision of services (electronic and other) to the user?
		Lifelong learner (user)
		• Personal development
		• Reflection
		• Finding learning
		• Engaging with:
		  • learning support
		  • peers
		  • professional bodies
		• Accessing multiple sources of information
		• Personal presentation

2. Clarify purpose of the solution	What services could be improved? (increasing benefit or reducing cost) What gaps exist in provision of services? (less likely) What problem does the application solve?	• Current eSystems • Current manual systems

Plan Benefits		
Action	**Questions**	**Factors**
3. Define functionality	What functions will provide the benefit the user needs? What other special benefits come from the solution?	• Individual functions • New integrated functionality • Speed of transaction or reporting • Interaction with peers • Interaction with customers • Interaction with suppliers
4. Identify functionality from existing provision that can be incorporated into the eSystem	What is already in existence that provides the required benefits?	• Access to external related functionality • Portability of data

Avoiding Costs		
Action	**Questions**	**Factors**
5. Identify security requirement	What are the legal requirements? What are the personal requirements?	
6. Design stability	Where will the eSystem be hosted; is it stable enough and supported for the required life of the solution?	
7. Evaluate affordability	How does the price of the solution compare to current provision?	

Planning the User Experience		
Action	**Questions**	**Factors**
8. Design logical function	What are the logical steps involved in performing the function(s)? What alternative logical path(s) could be provided?	
9. Design intuitiveness	What interfaces will the user be familiar with? How can the application be designed to make the user feel at home?	• User's prior experience with software (e.g. MS Word, Google, Amazon) • User's experience with non-IT interfaces (e.g. cash machines, TVs, traffic lights)
10. Design clarity of communication	How clear is it where 'clickable items are'? How clear is it what the impact of using a certain part of the interface is? How cluttered is the interface with different messages?	• Use of language • Written clarification of steps • Tool tips appearing on hover • Simplicity
11. Design navigation	How easy is it to move from one part of the system to another? How easy is it to retrace steps? How is data maintained between screen changes?	• Multiple intelligences
12. Design visual appearance	How does it look? What feelings will the look of the system generate for the user?	• Colours • Font size • Graphic design • Simplicity • 'Form follows function'
13. Create accessibility	What provision is there for disabled users with accessibility needs? What are the legal requirements for accessibility?	

Plan User Support		
Action	**Questions**	**Factors**
14. Provide training	What training will the user require? How will training be provided for the user?	• Help • eLearning • Trainers
15. Provide support	What will happen if an error occurs on the system? Who is responsible for maintaining the application?	• Error handling • Clear error messages
16. Provide feedback opportunity	How can a user feed back problems?	

Useful Websites

Here is a list of websites which may be of use for further research into developing eSystems with user value:

www.cogent-ssc.com

www.engc.org.uk

www.fdf.ac.uk

www.gfk.com/

www.heacademy.ac.uk

www.hull.ac.uk/cpd-eng/

www.jisc.ac.uk

www.internetworldstats.com

www.itu.int/en/pages/default.aspx

www.pd-how2.org

www.sflqi.org.uk

CHAPTER THIRTEEN

YHELLN's Legacy and Lessons Learnt

Kath Bridger

In June 2004 the Higher Education Funding Council for England (HEFCE) set out its intention to 'make a step change in vocational progression' through the development of Lifelong Learning Networks (LLNs). The first group of LLNs were established in September 2005 and in the Humber sub-region YHELLN was established in January 2007. HEFCE defined their objective for LLNs as:

> to improve the coherence, clarity and certainty of progression opportunities for vocational learners into and through higher education.

HEFCE identified specific key areas for the focus of LLN activity in order to achieve their overall objective, namely, curriculum development to facilitate progression; information, advice and guidance and learner support systems; and network-wide progression agreements.

In order to take this work forward, YHELLN built on the long-established history of collaboration between the further and higher education sectors in the sub-region. YHELLN's core delivery partners were:

- Bishop Burton College (nr Beverley)
- Doncaster College
- East Riding College (Beverley and Bridlington)
- Hull College (Hull and Goole)
- Grimsby Institute

- North Lindsey College (Scunthorpe)

- Selby College

- University of Hull (Hull and Scarborough)

- Yorkshire Coast College (Scarborough).

It is interesting to note that there was only one university in the partnership. YHELLN also worked with other stakeholders across the region, including Aimhigher, Higher York LLN and the Humber Education Business Partnership.

In addition to addressing HEFCE requirements, the establishment of YHELLN and the development of its business plan took account of local economic need. It focused, therefore, on four key sectors for the area, being engineering and construction; health, education and social care; business and logistics; and creative arts (including digital media). It also went on to include employer engagement as a key area for action in response to changing national agendas.

As is reflected among other LLNs nationally, the development of YHELLN was contingent on the environment in which it operated. The number and size of FE partners and the presence of a single University necessitated an approach which ensured there was no 'competition' between FE colleges, that need was met and that the University was able to respond appropriately to the facilitation of the progression of vocational learners. As part of gaining meaningful buy-in to both its business plan and its operational delivery, YHELLN ensured that it strategically aligned with all partners. This was helped by an acceptance that the degree of alignment would vary, reflecting the differing contexts and institutional priorities and drivers within each partner. In turn, partners recognised that their own strategic drivers influenced the type and extent of project activity they undertook making it relevant and beneficial to their own context. There was a good spread of activity and distribution of funding across all partners.

Whilst FE and HE are not strangers to partnership in the sub-region, the inclusive nature of the YHELLN network served to iterate and further develop trust and respect amongst its members. This, together with the support of financial resource, allowed the testing of new ways of working together, the taking of calculated risks and the capitalising on new opportunities for the developing of new approaches to progression, curriculum development and learner support. Indeed, the financial resource provided by YHELLN was a key factor in engaging the proactive participation of partners in developing the vocational progression agenda.

In addition, networking across external stakeholders proved to be a valuable means of both identifying new opportunities for developing vocational engagement in higher education and increasing awareness and understanding of higher education and higher level skills. The result was greater engagement of external agencies and organisations, both statutory and private sector, in the work of the YHELLN network to ensure vocational progression. This included work at a regional as well as sub-regional level through, for example, the development of the Logistics Academy and partnership working with the other LLNs in Yorkshire & the Humber. This has led to a greater profile for both the regional and sub-regional 'offer' in respect of vocational progression to higher education, as well as increased opportunities for learners.

Importantly, YHELLN clearly exceeded all targets set out within its business and operational plans and delivered above expectation, particularly in respect of curriculum development and progression agreements. Achieving targets was essential, both in terms of justifying the investment of public money by HEFCE and also in demonstrating to the partners the value they have gained from the partnership and in encouraging them to continue. In addition, there are significant direct and indirect benefits and impacts that can be identified resulting from its operation. It has been recognised that the expertise of YHELLN staff has been a key factor in this. The team succeeded in identifying and capitalising on new opportunities, developing progression agreements, curriculum initiatives and learner support which have resulted in the engagement of staff at all levels across partners, increased knowledge and understanding of vocational progression and a greater capacity to deliver real opportunities for vocational learners to progress and succeed. This has been equally as important as the progress made against hard targets, demonstrating to partners the beneficial impact of the cultural change which lay behind the measured achievements and ensuring their continuation in the future.

It will be important for the Federation, the body succeeding YHELLN, to maintain the inclusive nature of the partnership that has been engendered by YHELLN. It needs to continue to provide opportunities for colleagues to share their expertise and knowledge and facilitate further collaborative working for the benefit of learners.

What is also clear is that the fruition of YHELLN activity across all work strands is only now becoming apparent. As is not uncommon with time-bound project initiatives, initial development and delivery of the LLN were delayed as a result of recruitment difficulties. The network was, therefore, not fully operational until eight months into its three-year lifespan. This had a 'knock on' effect in respect of visible impact, particularly in terms of cultural change to facilitate and embrace vocational progression. The significance of the impact of YHELLN is only now emerging and, indeed, it may never be fully identified.

Reported increases in students progressing locally into higher education now appear to be borne out by statistics. Analysis of quantitative data to date indicates that there is a significant increase in progression to the University of Hull from students resident in the region. The number of applications to the University went up by 4 per cent for the academic year 2008/9, with an increase of 24 per cent for the current academic year 2009/10. Whilst this substantial increase cannot be directly attributed as a direct outcome of YHELLN, it is important to note that it coincides with the culmination of its activity.

Students have clearly benefited from the work that YHELLN undertook in a number of contexts – the promotion of clear progression pathways; appropriate IAG; learners support mechanisms; innovative and relevant curriculum. Aspirations were raised and students grew in confidence and achieved what they previously considered to be out of their reach. This was particularly the case for non-traditional students, including work-based learners and apprentices. As highlighted above, the factors which have facilitated this change are now becoming embedded within partner institutions.

The development and formalisation of progression agreements can be regarded as a key factor here – 75 had been signed off by December 2009 (the target had been 30 over the lifetime of the LLN). This formalisation of progression as a progression agreement, whether in relation to the recognition of a new progression arrangement or an existing informal arrangement, ensured that the progression opportunity was embedded and remains part of a review and evaluation process, thereby keeping it firmly on an institution's operational agenda.

The process for achieving a formalised progression agreement has proved to be as valuable as the agreement itself. The development of both internal and external progression agreements has instigated discussion within partner institutions which have led to increased knowledge and awareness in respect of progression and how it can successfully take place. This occurred across all staff, from practitioners / academic teaching staff to senior managers at departmental and institutional level. Further, developmental discussions and the implementation of progression agreements led to interventions to encourage learners to progress, from mentor support and additional and appropriate IAG to learner support tool kits and bespoke study skills modules.

In continuing to provide appropriate and robust opportunities for vocational learners, the development of progression agreements should continue to be rolled out to ensure that (a) more progression routes are identified and formalised and (b) the process of building relationships and understanding continues. The Federation is well placed to ensure that this happens by working across the partnership to roll out good practice and identify new areas for development.

Progression agreement development has been supported by the development of innovative curriculum. This has demonstrated what is possible in terms of context, course content, delivery and assessment to secure meaningful vocational progression. A good example of this is a work-based certificate programme developed by the University's Centre for Lifelong Learning for Kimberly-Clark and leading to progression to the University's Business Leadership and Management programme. This also demonstrated an excellent model of employer engagement to develop higher level skills in the workplace.

The development of Foundation degrees facilitated the successful development of models of more proactive employer engagement. This resulted in programmes of study which meet the needs of industry and the learner through the development of understanding between employers and education practitioners. Feedback from employers, colleges and the University and the learners themselves was positive and indicates the benefit of these developments.

Possibly the most significant curriculum development initiative has been Staged Engagement which has provided a new model of practice in the development and delivery of a flexible approach to higher education, relevant in multiple contexts and embraced by all partners. This model is continuing to be employed by all partners and provides a legacy product by which YHELLN will certainly be remembered.

In moving forward, drawing on the innovative and successful models of practice developed, the continuation of appropriate curriculum developments can be assured through the Federation, thus meeting the needs of the local economy to achieve a higher-level skills base and providing opportunities for vocational and work-based learners to successfully access and achieve in higher education.

The learner-centric approach of YHELLN ensured that in addition to developing appropriate, innovative curriculum and the means to progress through it being in place, learner support formed a key aspect of its delivery. The Learner Support Strand of activity operated alongside Curriculum Development and Progression work. The close working practices that were forged between the three Work Strand Managers ensured that learner support was embedded as an integral part of progression and curriculum development. Joint working across these strands highlighted gaps in appropriate learner support provision and resulted in the development of initiatives to provide interventions to facilitate progression and the retention of vocational learners, for example, study skills resources including a maths package for Business Studies students. This type of development can be replicated for other specific curriculum areas. All aspects of learners' entitlement to IAG and appropriate support were addressed in order to ensure that it is sustained within progression and curriculum development, enabling students to fulfil their potential through a quality student experience.

The strategy employed by YHELLN to build capacity within partner organisations in respect of learner support rather than the direct delivery of IAG was widely recognised as beneficial and regarded as a sustainable impact. IAG staff now reflect that they feel better equipped to offer more appropriate advice and a better quality of service to learners as a result of access to staff development opportunities in respect of IAG and learner support, particularly the NVQs in Information, Advice and Guidance, and through the consultancy guidance offered in respect of the implementation of IAG quality standards.

The implementation of a statement of Learner Entitlement in respect of IAG, signed at senior management level within each partner institution, ensured that the provision of quality, appropriate information, advice and guidance was strategically placed and a commitment made to its delivery ensuring that it can be embedded in policy and practice.

The commitment at institutional and individual levels to the delivery of an entitlement to quality IAG and learner support for all students needs to be iterated in all policy, procedure and practice developments across all partner institutions in order that it remains embedded. This could be achieved by ensuring that it forms a key aspect of the approach to vocational progression and the recruitment and retention of a diverse student population through the Federation moving forward. Where gaps are identified, additional research should be undertaken in order to further increase the understanding of the needs of vocational learners and develop evidence informed practice.

As alluded to above, an increase in awareness and understanding amongst staff of vocational progression and the needs of vocational learners can be identified as a significant outcome of the work of YHELLN. A variety of both formal and informal opportunities for staff development succeeded in building capacity within partner organisations. Formal opportunities included both accredited and non accredited provision and access to CPD activity. Informal development resulted from the networking and relationship building which formed a key aspect of progression, curriculum development, learner support and research activities.

Informal staff development was significant in its impact on staff attitudes and approaches to learning, teaching and assessment in respect of a diverse student population. Staff, particularly at individual and departmental level, widened their understanding of the needs of vocational learners and developed their curriculum offer and practice accordingly.

Formal CPD opportunities had a variable impact which would appear to stem from the differential levels of engagement by partners. This can be attributed to the different needs of multiple partners and also the recognition of the relevance of the offer made. Where a specific need for direct impact on practice was identified, formal opportunities were most successful, e.g. NVQs in Advice and Guidance which were welcomed by staff and enabled them to develop their practice in IAG.

In addition, the range of research activity undertaken by YHELLN not only provided a valuable academic resource for future developments but also informal CPD opportunities for staff who would not readily have access to participating in this type of scholarly activity. Dissemination of the outputs provided further opportunities for staff.

CPD and staff development opportunities should be maintained in order to sustain cultural change and build capacity, taking both an informal and formal approach across partners. This should include the exploration of further research opportunities, both in partnership and by individual institutions in order to strengthen the evidence base for the development of best and successful practice in respect of vocational learners and a diverse student body. The Federation is well placed to ensure that cross-institutional opportunities are developed and promoted and can be accessed by staff at all levels in order to improve practice and ensure best learner outcomes.

Whilst not an initial priority area for action, YHELLN made significant progress in taking forward the employer engagement agenda in respect of vocational progression and the development of relevant curriculum and qualifications, successfully securing employer buy-in and input. The benefits, including greater efficiency, addressing skills needs and the recruitment of staff, are recognised by employers who are now becoming advocates of sector-specific, work-related higher-level skills development. The models of employer engagement developed through the above work are replicable and can form the basis of future work with employers.

YHELLN's ability to respond to changing agendas, e.g. employer engagement, and tap into external strategic opportunities benefited all partners and enhanced their capacity to deliver an appropriate offer for both industry and vocational learners. The spin-off activity that emerged demonstrated this impact, e.g. knowledge transfer activity; Logistics Academy; Professional Engineering Centre.

By demonstrating what is possible in the arena of higher level skills and vocational progression YHELLN succeeded in creating a momentum for change at all levels. Strategically, it fired the debate about vocational progression, the need to recognise the value of a diverse student population which includes vocational learners and the actions which need to be taken to support them; within departments and faculties there has been recognition that the curriculum offer needs to be relevant and flexible and needs to take account of the background and experience of potential students in order to facilitate progression; the development of understanding and, consequently, in practice at individual practitioner level has produced advocates and champions for innovative and inclusive proactive development. Student entitlement has become a key point of reference which needs to be further promoted and secured.

Although the entire extent of YHELLN's footprint across the vocational progression agenda may never be fully equated, what is clear is that it has had a significant impact on the partners involved, the Humber sub-region and more widely across the Yorkshire & Humber region. It will leave a legacy of products and effective practice and the emergence of a positive cultural shift in attitudes to work-based and vocational progression to higher education.

An Accountant's Reflections

Glen Jack

At the end of November 2006 my wife and I (and two cats) loaded up our car and headed for Hull. We had previously proposed and rejected the Isle of Skye (too far and cold and dark), Brigg (because my mate lived there) and staying put in London (too expensive and busy). So Hull it was.

My wife already had a job offer at Hull College, but I was throwing myself onto the motorway of fate and seeing what was going to hit me. What hit me was YHELLN.

My recent past employment history was with local government in London looking after a big budget, so although I had not worked in education before my interview with YHELLN, obviously they came to the conclusion that 'numbers are numbers' and I would be OK for the role.

I took up the Management Accountant post in April 2007 and inherited an almost blank canvas as far as monitoring and reporting of the finances were concerned. There had been a small amount of expenditure prior to my arrival (set up costs etc) and there existed the original and updated budgets, but I saw it as my initial role to formulate reporting processes and systems from our partners to the centre and from the centre to the Management and Steering Groups.

The structure of YHELLN was such that each of our eight partners would have a support officer (either full time or part time) who would administrate matters within their respective colleges, part of which would be the ordering and paying of YHELLN reclaimable expenditure. To monitor this I devised a spreadsheet with some simple formulas that would allow the support officers to keep track of what had been spent and report to me on a monthly/quarterly basis. I also contacted all our partners' finance departments to both introduce myself and request that they render retrospective quarterly invoices to me for their expenditure (salaries, travel etc). Also within the YHELLN structure were four work strands, each with a budget. Again, it needed a simple spreadsheet with expenditure reducing the budget balance when entered and monitored against profile.

The final piece of the reporting jigsaw was the management accounts showing the overall position year on year, the overall budget showing the yearly actual and projections and the monthly management letter to the Director and subsequently the Management and Steering Groups, outlining the financial position. I also 'presented' the financial position at all Management and Steering Groups. All we needed now were staff in place to spend the money!

Lesson 1: Staff won't join as per profile

Originally, the budget had allowed for all staff to be in place by the end of the financial year 31 July 2007. In reality, only the Directorate, myself and one support officer were in post by the end of July and it would take till February 2008 to achieve full staffing levels. This had a knock-on effect in that, apart from MLE/website and Communications and Marketing, there was no spend within the work strand budgets. There was also an underspend against the projected running costs (stationery, travel), mainly because there was no-one around to write or travel!

Lesson 2: Be financially flexible

With regard to the work strand budgets, the totals available remained the same but now with a truncated profile. This would remain the mantra as year-on-year spend didn't ever quite catch up, yet the financial outcomes remained constant throughout the life of YHELLN, or until it was decided to divert these budgets into other areas. As regards the office and salary first year underspend, that would be retained until a decision by the Steering Group as to its financial destination.

It became clear that YHELLN was falling behind the original HEFCE receipt profile which pleased the University of Hull (as bankers) no end, but not our funding body. A cessation of payments by HEFCE was agreed and the remaining funds re-profiled to lessen the current 'cash in hand'. A re-jigged spending profile was also put into place and all seemed set fair for receipts and spend to dovetail from here on in. However...

Lesson 3: It can be hard to spend money!!

Astonishingly, quite a large part of my working week was taken up chasing invoices or reminding partners to send me invoices or to rectify incorrect invoices. At one point, one of our partner colleges was nine months (three quarters) outstanding – a not insignificant amount of funds. It exacerbated the problem of ensuring that YHELLN achieved a zero outturn on the budget, as I was never quite sure of what expenditure some partners were incurring against specific budget lines.

By the end of September 2009 all our partners were up to date, running cost (salary and office expenditure) wise, but with the project reaching its close, YHELLN faced another problem...

Lesson 4: Staff won't leave as per profile

YHELLN staff were divided between those on fixed term contracts (to 31 December 2009) and those staff members who were seconded. The split was roughly two-thirds fixed term and one-third seconded, so there clearly was a high risk should staff leave, especially as all but one of the Directorate were on fixed term contracts.

The first staff member to leave did so in August 2008 and by December 2008 a further two staff members had left. None of these roles were subsequently filled, as it was decided that their workloads could be subsumed into the existing capacity, but also it was felt that the time it would take to advertise and appoint to these roles would make any contractual offers unappealing.

A risk assessment of staff attrition and its impact on the YHELLN Operational Plan was drawn up to highlight where posts could be covered either by existing resources or by using consultants, or where posts posed a high risk due to the nature of the role and/or the inability to be covered either internally or externally. Each post was rated as to the 'likelihood' of the incumbent leaving, based on whether the staff member had indicated if they were actively engaged in searching for a new post or not, and how transferable the skills of staff members were to fulfil any roles available within the current labour market.

It had always been expected that, as the YHELLN closure date grew nearer staff would leave, especially as the last six to nine months approached. In truth, this was not the case. Only a further two posts became vacant and those only within August/September 2009. Some staff were offered alternative roles, both internally and externally, but they would not commence until January 2010.

I think it is fair to say that the current economic recession played a major role in staff not moving from YHELLN. The labour market nationally is fairly stagnant and within the YHELLN geographical area this is equally so. Staff on University of Hull contracts were placed on the redeployment list with varying degrees of success, whilst we hoped that staff within our partners' institutions would be offered employment. At the time of writing this does not appear probable.

Lesson 5: Spend, spend, spend

As can be seen by the preceding 'lessons', YHELLN had an underspend that was building yearly. Initially, funds had remained 'uncommitted', as the intention had been to sustain YHELLN (or certain parts of it) after the end date of 31 December 2009. Further to this, YHELLN would seek to obtain external funding to supplement the existing funds. However, around the end of 2008 the Steering Group decided not to agree to a continuation of the Network but to subsume the work of YHELLN within an existing structure (the Federation). This left the problem of what to do with uncommitted funds.

After consultation with both the YHELLN Steering and Management groups, it was decided to commission a range of projects across the partnership which had a total funding of £436,000. All projects had to be completed by mid-December and to manage this risk a 'traffic lights' system of monitoring the projects was implemented with monthly meetings by a panel to ensure all timetables and milestones were adhered to.

As further uncommitted funds became available, project extensions were funded, allowing the system to react to any underspends, whilst still retaining the mid- December deadlines. To date, YHELLN has funded over 100 projects, representing a substantial financial and logistical commitment.

At the end of the financial year 2008–9 (July 2009) YHELLN had spent just over two-thirds of the overall budget which meant that £1,092,269 would be spent in the last five months of the life of the network. The main areas of this spend were salaries and projects, but all expenditure at time of writing is committed and the target of a zero outturn remains a realistic outcome.

In conclusion

On 31 December 2009 YHELLN will put out the lights, close the doors and staff will go their various ways.

Like all of life experiences, I have learnt from being involved with YHELLN and, hopefully, I can use the knowledge gained in any future role(s).

There can be no doubt that YHELLN has been successful, as I am sure other contributors to this book will have enunciated far better than I ever could. If, however, we spend all £3.9 million to achieve those successes and if the initiatives and resources that YHELLN has created can be sustained, then the personal and professional satisfaction that I have had whilst working for YHELLN will have reached a suitable conclusion.

Now, back onto the motorway of fate.

Bibliography

Archer, L., Hutchings, M. and Ross. A., *Higher education and social class: issues of inclusion and exclusion*. Routledge, 2003.

Ball, S.J. and Vincent, C (1998) 'I heard it on the grapevine: "hot" knowledge and school choice. *British Journal of Sociology of Education* 19 (3) 377–400.

BIS, *Building Britain's digital future: action plan for the digital economy*. BIS, 2009.

Bloom, B.S. (ed.) *Taxonomy of Educational Objectives: The Classification of Educational Goals*. Longman, 1955.

Bolton, J.E., Small firms, report of the Committee of Inquiry on small firms, HMSO, 1971.

Branden, N., *The psychology of self-esteem: a revolutionary approach to self-understanding that launched a new era in modern psychology*. Jossey-Bass, 2001.

Collins Concise English Dictionary. Collins, 2008.

Curtis, P., 'Government working with Tory grandee on technical school revival'. *Guardian*, 31 August 2009, p.9.

Curtis, P., 'League table plan for all universities'. *Guardian*, 23 October 2009, p.1.

Dearing, R., 'The Challenges and Opportunities facing the University'. Keynote address to the University of Hull Learning and Teaching Conference, 17 January 2008 (unpublished).

Denham, J., *Universities must work together with business to encourage mature students into Higher Education*. DIUS, 2007.

DfES, Information, Advice and guidance for Adults – national policy framework and Action Plan. DfES 2003.

DIUS, *World Class Skills: Implementing the Leitch Review of Skills*. DIUS, 2007.

Doyle, P., *Marketing Management and Strategy*. Prentice Hall, 1998.

Drucker, P.F., *Management tasks, responsibilities and practices*. Heinemann, 1974.

Ewell, P.T., *Organizing for learning: A point of entry*. Draft prepared for discussion at the 1997 AAHE Summer Academy at Snowbird. National Centre for Higher Education Management Systems (NCHEMS).

Franz, R. S., 'Whatever you do, don't treat your students like customers!'. *Journal of Management Education*, 22 (1), 1998, pp.63–69.

Fuller-Love, N.,' Management development in small firms'. *International Journal of Management Reviews*, 8 (3), 2006, pp.175–90.

Gallacher, J., Written evidence to the Scottish Parliament 'Some issues for consideration the contribution of education and training to business growth in Scotland'. www.scottish.parliament.uk, 2005.

Haywood, M., Nixon, I., Bell, R., and Burke, J., 'Evaluation and Review of Technical Developments to Support Lifelong Learning'. JISC,www.jisc.ac.uk, April 2009.

HMSO, Disability and Discrimination Act. HMSO, 2005.

HMSO, Special Educational Needs and Disability Act (SENDA). HMSO, 2001.

Hutchings, M., 'Information, advice and cultural discourses of higher education' in Archer et al, *Higher education and social class: issues of inclusion and exclusion*. Routledge, 2003.

Johnson, G., Scholes, K. and Whittington, R., *Exploring Corporate Strategy*, 7th edition. Pearson Education, 2005.

Johnson, S., 'Lifelong Learning and SMEs: issues for research and policy'. *Journal of Small Business and Enterprise Development*, Vol.9 No.3, 2002, pp.285–95.

Kehrwald, B., 'Learners' Experiences with Learner Support in Networked Learning Communities'. Paper presented at the 6th International Conference on Lifelong Learning, 2008. www.networkedlearningconference.org.uk/abstracts/PDFs/Kehrwald 210–217.pdf.

Knapper, C.K., Cropley, A.J., *Lifelong Learning in Higher Education*. Routledge; 1991.

Leitch, S., *Prosperity for all in the global economy – world class skills*.

London: HM Treasury, 2006.

LSC, *Providers, money to learn – learner support service, Resources to help you*. LSC, 2009.

Lunnan, R., and Haugland, S., 'Predicting and Measuring Alliance Performance: a Multidimensional Analysis'. *Strategic Management Journal*, 29, 2008, pp.545–56.

Maclellan, E., Conceptual Learning: The Priority for Higher Education, British Journal of Educational Studies, 53 (2), 2005 pp.129–47.

Newby, H., 'Lifelong learning networks in higher education'. *Journal of Access Policy and Practice* 2 (2), 2005 pp.176–86.

Parise, S. and Sasson, L., 'Leveraging Knowledge Management Across Strategic Alliances'. *Ivey Business Journal*, 66 (4), Mar/Apr 2002.

Rammell, B. *Higher Education at Work, High Skills: High Value*. DIUS, 2008.

Reed, J. and Sowden, D., 'E-systems development within Lifelong Learning Networks', 2008, found at: www.lifelonglearningnetworks.org.uk/documents/document378. pdf.

SummitSkills, *Foundation Degree Framework Specification for the Building Services Engineering Sector VI*. SummitSkills, October 2008.

Tight, M., 'Education, Education, Education! The Vision of Lifelong Learning in the Kennedy, Dearing and Fryer Reports'. *Oxford Review of Education*, 24 (4), 1998, pp.473–85.

Wedgewood, M., *Higher Education for the Workforce – Barriers and Facilitators to Employment Engagement*. DIUS, January 2008.

Whitston, K., 'HEFCE has invested £100 million in 28 networks in Lifelong Learning Networks'. HEFCE, 2007.

Willis, P., *Learning to Labour: How working class kids get working class jobs*. Saxon House, 1977.

Wolf, A., *Does Education Matter? Myths about education and economic growth*. Penguin, 2002.

Contributor Biographies

Jane Barker

Jane is a qualified teacher who moved into Careers, Education and Guidance in 1986. The experience in schools led onto working for the then newly formed North Yorkshire Business and Education Partnership in 1992, creating and managing many varied projects between both local and national business and schools and colleges in the county. The role with NYBEP also included delivering and organising the teacher placement service on behalf of North Yorkshire and also managing the North East England Regional teacher placement network for a number of years. Jane moved onto the Connexions service in 2002 as a 14–19 Education Manager from where she was seconded to YHELLN to facilitate and manage the Learner Support/IAG projects. Whilst at YHELLN Jane concentrated on capacity building for Learner Support/IAG professionals through a variety of training initiatives and programmes together with creating a labour market information website www.lmiyny.co.uk for the county of York and North Yorkshire. She has since returned to working with VT Enterprises concentrating on the Adult Guidance area.

Lynn Benton

When this book was written, Lynn Benton was the coordinator for Yorkshire and Humber Lifelong Learning Network. Her experience covers 36 years of working within organisations associated with all aspects of learning and skills. Lynn's experience covers Skills for Life, 14–19 provision and all aspects of Community Learning and she has worked with public, voluntary and community organisations to develop and manage a wide range of learning opportunities that have been aimed at widening participation in all aspects of learning. Lynn has been involved in research regarding skills and learning, which has formed the basis of a number of strategies and plans that she has written for local authorities. Lynn chairs a board of Trustees for a Charity and has also chaired a board of Directors for a Company Limited by Guarantee, so her experience also covers voluntary and community organisations that deliver learning opportunities and support to both young people and adults. Lynn has a BA in Librarianship and a Masters in Business Administration from the University of Hull, as well as NVQ Level 4 in Management.

Kath Bridger

Kath is a freelance consultant with a strong background in the higher education sector. She has held senior posts in the UK higher education sector (including the Interim Directorship of the Yorkshire and Humber East LLN, and Director of Access and Widening Participation at the University of Bradford). She has worked extensively as a consultant across the public, private and voluntary sectors, supporting organisations to develop their business and partnership strategies and facilitating the development of inclusive policy and business practice. This has included review and evaluation of equality and diversity policy and practice, and for some clients developing more inclusive approaches to learning and access to learning. Kath was co-researcher on the HEA funded research project 'Embedding Widening Participation and Promoting Student Diversity. What can be learned from a business case approach?' and most recently 'Developing and Embedding Inclusive Policy and Practice in Higher Education' (Higher Education Academy, 2010). Kath carried out the Evaluation and Impact Assessment for YHELLN.

Andrew Chandler

Andrew studied Plant Biology at the University of Hull in the mid-70s, returning to the South West after graduating in order to train as a careers adviser. He spent five years in Plymouth working as an adviser with a range of clients, before moving to Essex to manage the Careers Centre in Rayleigh. In 1987, Andrew moved to Hull to work for the Careers Service in Humberside and was responsible for managing a range of support services and ICT projects. In 1997, he joined the Chartered Institute of Marketing and took on responsibility for business development activities as well as the development of the service's (now privatised) marketing plans/strategies. During periods of secondment, Andrew has worked for the Department for Education and Skills as a consultant on a young people's internet portal project and with a software company in Edinburgh to develop an internet-based CRM MIS solution as a support system for Connexions personal advisers. After being made redundant in 2005, he joined igen Ltd as 'nextstep' Contract Manager and managed the adult guidance contract in the Humber region, awarded by the Learning and Skills Council, before leaving to become Communications Manager at the Yorkshire & Humber East Lifelong Learning Network until December 2009.

John Deverell

After graduating from Queen Mary College, London with an Electrical Engineering degree, John Deverell worked at AERE Harwell for five years before teaching in Higher Education. He was a Principal Lecturer for thirty-three years at the University of Lincolnshire and Humberside and held various Head of Department roles in the Faculty of Technology. His main interest was in curriculum development, particularly for the accredited BEng awards run in the Faculty. He had a particular interest in the promotion of these awards for part-time students in the Humberside area. He was an active member of both the Institute of Electrical Engineering and the Institute of Measurement and Control and was a QAA Assessor in Electrical Engineering.

Sarah Gribbin

Sarah is a lecturer in Leadership and Management in the Faculty of Health and Social Care in the University of Hull. With professional life that spans the private and public sector, academic roles, senior management, consultancy and research, Sarah has a wide range of skills and experience. Her teaching areas include strategy, innovation and change, knowledge transfer and consultancy. She has experience of international higher education and UK Further Education. She has also worked for large plcs as well as SMEs. Her experience includes strategy development, public sector, evaluation of projects, management of higher education, skills development, charity sector, food industry, retail, employer engagement, the logistics sector, partnership working, establishment of new initiatives, bid writing and mentoring.

Nick Hooper

After achieving First Class Honours in Social Sciences (Economics) at the University of Bradford, Nick began his career as a Statistician with the National Economic Development Office. He followed this with a spell as an Industrial Development Analyst with the State oil company in Saudi Arabia. Returning to the UK, he continued his involvement with the Middle East as a consultant. A contract from the Ministry of Defence took him to the University of York, where he stayed for 12 years, helping to develop the Centre for Defence Economics into an internationally recognised centre of expertise. After a spell at Leeds Metropolitan University undertaking research, Nick returned to consultancy for a wide variety of clients. Joining the University of Hull he ran a Consortium developing and delivering skills for life professional training, before joining YHELLN as Work Strand Manager for Research, CPD and Evaluation. He is the author of over 50 books and articles on industrial economics and has presented his work at international conferences, and in press, on TV and in radio interviews. He is currently working part time in the Centre for Leadership, Innovation and Change through Knowledge Transfer in the Faculty of Health and Social Care, University of Hull.

Sarah Humphreys

Sarah undertook an MA (Electronic Arts) at Middlesex University, specialising in Interactive Media, prior to establishing the New Media area at Hull School of Art and Design where she has resumed her role as Curriculum Leader following a secondment with Yorkshire and Humber East Lifelong Learning Network as Higher Skills Team Leader for Creative Arts. Sarah is experienced in curriculum development and is actively engaged in furthering an extensive Higher Education provision for the School. Sarah is an external examiner, held a three-year Teacher Fellowship, and in 2004 was nominated for a National Teacher Fellowship. Sarah's areas of interest are the development of interactive online environments for archiving and curation, for exhibition and to support learning. She has managed a numbers of projects including the European Illustration Collection Hull, Hull Short Film Study resource, the Digital Studio and most recently an online portfolio/jobs resource. She has written about digital environments for the arts in a range of journals and conference publications.

Glen Jack

My two and a half years with YHELLN was one of the most pleasant working experiences of my life (so far). I had previously spent five years with the London Borough of Camden within the Planning Department, rising to the dizzy heights of Principal Finance Officer, a title that sounds slightly grander that it actually was but I did have lots of money to take care of! Prior to Camden I had been Musical Director for Saga Shipping. That basically meant I told ten musicians what they were doing each day and guided all the artistes and production shows through the musical minefield that was rehearsal and performance culminating in a standing ovation and a round of drinks. I like reading, playing golf, cheering on Chelsea Football Club (via Sky Sports), and listening to my wife! I am currently studying maths at Hull College for no other reason than Thursday night's a bit duff on telly.

Laura Minghella

Laura worked for YHELLN as the Support Officer based at Yorkshire Coast College. She worked closely with Jane Barker during the operation of YHELLN on the IAG strand of activity.

Karen Quine

Dr Karen Quine gained her EdD from The University of Derby in 2008 focusing on Action Research in a manufacturing organisation. Prior to this Karen gained her MA in Marketing Management from the University of Hull. She has extensive knowledge of teaching and managing in both the Further and Higher Education sector and has been Programme Manager for Postgraduate provision at Dearne Valley Business School. Prior to this Karen was Executive Manager for Higher Education at Dearne Valley College and was responsible for implementing the first directly funded HE provision within the FE College. Her most recent activity has been as Curriculum Development Manager for a Lifelong Learning Network which included working with partner colleges and universities in developing innovative curriculum models in line with current Government thinking and targets. Karen has a passion for lifelong learning and current interests include working closely with business in all Knowledge Transfer activities including KTPs, Organisational Learning and Development, Work Based Learning and Recognition of Prior Leaning Experiences.

Jason Reed

Jason is a management consultant experienced in Business, IT and Education. In practice he facilitates learning, innovation and collaboration and develops community engagement. Formerly he was the Managing Director of IT Interface, an IT solutions business that won the 'best trainer' award for the Yorkshire Forward vendor skills programme during 2004. He led the creation of the IT Interface joint venture in partnership with the University of Hull and was also a member of the board of Directors of the Humber New Technology Institute. He has worked extensively with Information Managers from large and small organisations, analysing their businesses, creating solutions and managing projects. This experience led him to found the Information Managers Group (IMG) based in the Humber region. Recently he has been working as a consultant in the development of educational systems at Yorkshire and Humber East Lifelong Learning Network (YHELLN) and as one of the main facilitators of global virtual teams innovating at www.ideaconnection.com.

Charlie Sanders

Charlie Sanders has held various senior posts in the further and higher Education Sector including Higher Education Curriculum Development Manager, Head of Department, Deputy to the Director of Higher Education, and Accreditation and Certificated Equivalence Manager at various local education institutions. More recently he has worked for the Yorkshire and Humber East Lifelong Learning Network as Progression Manager, with the aim of ensuring more vocational students in the Humber sub-region progress to higher education in vocational subject areas. As an experienced practitioner in the field of post-16 education he has wide knowledge of the issues and barriers revolving around the higher level skills gap. With wide experience of curriculum development and programme validation in both the further and higher education sectors, he has undertaken a number of research projects to enable skills shortages to be mapped at a variety of levels. Charlie has been instrumental in the development of vocationally based Foundation and Honours degrees and has also developed work-based Foundation degree programmes with local employers as part of the Higher Level skills agenda. This has allowed local employers flexibility of higher education provision through work-based and part-time programmes as a tool for upskilling their workforce. Charlie works at present as an Educational Consultant

Jenny Shaw

Jenny Shaw was Director of the Yorkshire and Humber East LLN between 2007 and 2009, and is now a freelance consultant and Director of BSV Associates Ltd. She has previously held senior posts in Aimhigher North Yorkshire and Middlesex University. As well as being an experienced practitioner in widening participation and business and community engagement in higher education, Jenny also has a profile as a published author and researcher. She holds a BSc (Hons) in Mathematics and Anthropology from the University of Durham. She lives in a small village in East Yorkshire with her husband and two daughters.

David Sowden

David has significant national expertise in learning technology in both HE and FE institutions and has contributed to national and international peer-reviewed conferences and publications in this field. He has led a major eSystems development for the Yorkshire and Humber East Lifelong Learning Network, including management of additional JISC funded projects to support eSystems for lifelong learners. During this time he played a leading role in the LLN National Forum eSystems Workstrand, promoting the use of common data standards, particularly XCRI, and championing usability and accessibility issues. He is currently managing at the University of Hull a JISC project in the Institutional Innovation projects in lifelong learning and workforce development funding round, developing 'smart' ePortfolio aggregator technology for professional engineers linked both to their programmes of work-based study from FD through to Masters, and also to their requirements as professionals to present their professional CPD profile both to employers, and to their professional body to gain professional status. David has a deep working knowledge of the potential and limitations of technology in supporting teaching, learning and the student experience in higher education, and draws perspectives from across the world to inform his work, particularly on usability and accessibility.